BUCKINGHAMSHIRE
MURDERS

LEN WOODLEY

The
Book
Castle

First Published September 1998
by
The Book Castle
12 Church Street
Dunstable
Bedfordshire LU5 4RU

ISBN 1 871199 93 X
Computer Typeset by Keyword, Aldbury, Herts.
Printed by Progressive Printing (UK) Ltd., Leigh-on-Sea, Essex.

Photos:
Front Cover: The Denham Murder
Frontispiece: Michael Bardell in custody
Back Cover: The grave of Pauline Alison Stevens

CONTENTS

ACKNOWLEDGEMENTS

I would like to express my appreciation to all those people who so willingly helped me in the preparation of this book, especially to those Police Officers, serving and retired who patiently answered my queries on the more recent murders described within. I would also like to acknowledge the assistance given me by so many others who either gave of their time to help me or who allowed me to intrude upon their privacy and take photographs of the various scenes of murders. I would also like to thank the Reverend A A Whalley of Newton Longville, the Reverend David Knight of Tysoe, Warwickshire, Mark Priddley of Oxfordshire Archives, Mrs Christine Mead, Marilyn Munn and Fay and Terry Rands of Dagnall, Derek Edmonds of Buckingham, The Meteorological Office, Richard Pearson of Denham, Iris Garrett and Jane Bird of Slough Museum, Mrs Batstone of Lent Green, Ann Brandon, Joe Elmes, Charles Clarkson and Mrs A Benwell of Great Horwood, the late Edward Ivory, ex-Detective Inspector Kenneth Savin, ex-Detective Chief Inspector Blackney Chambers, ex-Police Constable Stanley Swann B.E.M., John Bailey, Pickering (North Yorkshire) library, ex-Superintendent John Schofield, ex-Detective Chief Superintendent Keith Milner, former Detective Sergeant Terry Lee, ex-Detective Chief Superintendent Joseph Coffey, ex-Detective Chief Inspector John White, ex-Chief Superintendent Ken Diccox, Detective Constable Roy Neale of the Thames Valley Police, Northampton Reference Library, the Newspaper Library, Colindale, Thames Valley Police Welfare Office and finally my wife Mary for all her help.

SOURCES

Newspapers: *The Times, Daily Mail, Daily Mirror, News of the World, Daily Graphic, Daily Sketch, (London) Evening News, Morning Herald, Illustrated Police News, Northampton Mercury, Northampton Chronicle and Echo, Bucks Gazette, Buckinghamshire Advertiser, Buckingham Advertiser, Buckingham Express, South Bucks Free Press, Bucks Free Press, Bucks Advertiser, Bucks Herald, Bucks Examiner, Windsor Slough and Eton Express, Slough Observer, Malton Gazette, Hunts Post.*
Books: *The Hangman's Tale*, by Syd Dernley
        Most of My Murders, by John Parris

INTRODUCTON

Like my earlier book, Murder in Buckinghamshire, this is an anthology of murders which took place in that County, commencing with the early nineteenth century and proceeding up to the nineteen eighties. Once again I have taken the County of Buckingham to include those parts lost under the Local Government re-organisation of the nineteen seventies and therefore Slough, which is now geographically Berkshire, is also represented.

As the first cases unfold it must be realised that there were no professional Police Forces to investigate these crimes and it was left to the Parish Constable, examining magistrate or even the local populace to raise a 'Hue and Cry', and attempt to apprehend any wrongdoers. Gradually, during the nineteenth century, Police Forces were created, firstly in the towns, like Buckingham, which never had above four men at any one time, and High or Chepping Wycombe. Then in 1857 the Buckinghamshire Constabulary was formed to cover the more rural parts of the County. In 1889 Buckingham lost its little force and High Wycombe was taken over by the County in 1947. Just over twenty years later, under the biggest round of amalgamations ever seen in this country, Buckinghamshire was then absorbed into the Thames Valley Constabulary along with the County Constabularies of Oxfordshire and Berkshire and the borough forces of Oxford and Reading.

Some of the earlier murders may now, to our eyes, seem unsophisticated and even quaint but they all show a representation of society at that particular moment in time. All were brutal and unnecessary and tend to show human nature at its worst.

Dedicated to all the victims of the crimes described within this book.

Michael Bardell in custody.

THE CHANDLER and the CARPENTER

Newton Longville 1814

At twenty minutes to eight on the evening of Monday, 21st February, 1814 old Mr Verney (or Varney) served his very last customer at the chandler's shop he owned at Newton Longville. It was a boy who had been sent for some candles and as the young lad picked up his bundle and left the shop he closed the door, before scampering off into the cold darkness outside. In the shadows however, a man watched the boy until he disappeared from view. Glancing furtively about, with one hand stuck in his coat as though holding something, he entered the shop and quickly closed the door behind him, for he had something more serious on his mind than the purchase of candles.

The clock at nearby St. Faith's Church had struck eight as a man walking past the chandler's noticed that the door was ajar. As this was somewhat unusual he paused and looked more closely. As he did so he heard the sound of groaning coming from the interior of the shop. His curiosity was aroused but not,

The Old Forge at Newton Longville.

it seemed, his bravery, for he made off in the direction of the Red Lion public house where he gasped out his story to the astonished customers of that hostelry. A number of them left their drinks and went to the chandler's where they too heard the sound of moaning coming from behind the counter. Cautiously they looked over the top and saw old Verney lying on the floor terribly wounded. One of the men went for a doctor but there was little he could do to aid the man and Verney died shortly after. A post-mortem examination revealed that Verney had been struck repeatedly about the head. 'By the claw of a large hammer', was the doctor's opinion.

As can be imagined a hue and cry went through the village and several witnesses were found who recalled seeing one man loitering near the shop shortly before the murder took place; a journeyman carpenter by the name of John Matthews. One of the villagers had even called out, 'G'night Master Matthews', but had received no reply, which he considered odd as he knew him very well. Matthews was detained and brought before a local Justice and interrogated. He categorically denied being at that end of the village at the time sworn to by the witnesses and was reluctantly released.

The authorities pondered their next course of action and decided to write to London and ask for the aid of a Bow Street Officer. Accordingly, one of them, Bishop, was sent to their assistance.

In the meantime, another witness had been found who could say that he saw Matthews in the vicinity of the shop the night before the murder! It was decided to re-arrest Matthews, this time on his wedding day as he was actually walking up the path of the Church with his bride – 'an industrious lace maker'. When Bishop arrived the suspect was handed over to his custody. He searched Matthews and found a canvas bag containing twenty shillings and a further five shillings which Matthews had tried to conceal. At first it was thought that the money was counterfeit or 'bad' but it was proved to be suffering just the effects of having been hoarded. The Bow Street Officer asked him how he had come by the money and Matthews admitted obtaining the five shillings in change from Verney about a fortnight before the slaying. A son-in-law of the dead man said that Verney had been in possession of silver which gave the impression of being 'bad' similar to that in the possession of the suspect.

Questioning the local people, Bishop ascertained that Matthews had been out of work for three months prior to the murder and several thought that his intention to marry was extraordinary, as he would not be able to support a wife. However, on the morning after the killing he had bought a wedding ring, giving ten shillings in part payment; he had then paid twelve shillings for six gallons of beer for his wedding and had even ordered clothing amounting to £7 from a tailor.

On this evidence Matthews was committed to the Assizes but when the indictment was placed before the Grand Jury they recorded 'No True Bill' and the carpenter was released to find his way back to North Bucks.

There were no other suspects and the murder remained unsolved. However, one wonders if Matthews, as he passed the gallows on the outskirts of Newton Longville, ever gave an involuntary shudder as he considered his good fortune in not keeping an appointment with the hangman there early one March morning.

MURDER in a LONELY PLACE

Shabbington Wood 1816

Tysoe, arguably one of the prettiest villages in Warwickshire, lies at the foot of the Edge Hills which divide that county from Oxfordshire. The area, locally, is known as the Vale of the Red Horse, after the number of horses successively cut out of the rich light brown soil found here (since Saxon times). The village is supposed to derive its name from the Saxon god Tiw and was in fact seized from the Saxons at the time of the Conquest. Centuries later sheepherders taking their flocks from Wales to London passed through Tysoe, which accounts for its long meandering look. In 1642 the smell of bread, newly baked in the village, assailed the nostrils of the soldiers as they marched from nearby Compton Wynates to fight the first battle of the English Civil War at Edgehill. As late as the early nineteenth century apparently, there was a strong belief in witchcraft in the area, so much so that aged women were reluctant to use walking sticks as an aid as it was supposedly a notorious sign of a witch!

In October 1792 a son, Thomas, was born to Richard and Elizabeth Reason at Tysoe, (the surname is alternatively spelt Raisin). He was their second, and as soon as he was able Thomas worked for his father as a labourer until he reached the age of twelve. He was then apprenticed to a local butcher but went into service three years later when his master died. After two years he returned home and remained there for the next year but again went into service until he was twenty. Shortly after, Reason moved to Blackthorn on the Oxfordshire/Buckinghamshire border and married a local girl. Matrimonial life did not suit him, presumably through the age-old grounds for domestic strife – lack of money – for in 1816 Reason was committed for trial at Oxford Assizes for killing a sheep with intent to steal it. However upon examination by the Grand Jury, no true bill was found and Thomas was released.

It was barely seven days later, on the evening of April 13th when he called upon Mrs Elizbaeth Yorke, an old widow-woman who lived in a lonely house in Shabbington Wood near Oakley. Living with her at the time was Elizabeth Hawes, a relation, and Mrs Yorke's six year old grandson. After chatting through the evening Reason suddenly said that he wanted money. Mrs Yorke's immediate reaction was to tell him that she had none to give him. Reason then locked the door of the house and, pulling a clasp knife from his pocket, proceeded to cut the old woman's throat. So deeply did he plunge the knife into her that her head was almost severed from her body. Not satisfied with having inflicted such a fearsome wound which in itself would have been fatal, Reason then commenced beating her with a bar, which was used to fasten the window shutter, until she was quite dead.

Reason next turned his attention to Elizabeth Hawes who must have been in a frantic state of mind by now. He beat her savagely about the head and using the clasp knife cut her throat in two places leaving her for dead. Reason then ransacked the house in his search for money, eventually going upstairs. Miraculously Elizabeth Hawes had survived the ferocious attack and meanwhile managed to escape from the house of blood. Staggering through the wood, bleeding severely from the wounds inflicted on her and fainting several times, she endeavoured to reach the nearest house about three-quarters of a mile away.

Reason came downstairs and saw that one of the women he had attacked had made her getaway and immediately went in pursuit of her to finish the job. He stuck to the path and therefore missed her.

Elizabeth eventually reached her objective and burst in on the startled householder exclaiming, 'Oh, that cruel Reason!' and fainted once more. A doctor was sent for from Brill and on his arrival dressed her wounds and a deposition (statement) was then taken from her. A party of men returned to Mrs Yorke's house to find the old lady dead on the floor but the grandson still alive. Apparently in his haste Reason had overlooked the boy. An immediate hue and cry went up for the perpetrator and after an extensive search Reason was found hiding in the chimney of his father's house. He was detained,

THE FULL PARTICULARS OF THE

LIFE, TRIAL & EXECUTION,

OF

Thomas Raisin,

For the Murder of Elizabeth York, of Shabbington Wood in the Parish of Shabbington, in the County of Bucks.

Executed last Friday Morning in Front of the Town Hall, Aylesbury.

THOMAS RAISIN, the present subject, was born at Tysoe near Ridgway in Warwickshire, was brought up to work with his Father as a labourer till he attained the age of twelve years, he was then put an Apprentice to a Butcher, with whom he lived three years, when he left that business on account of his Master's death; he then went into a Gentlemans service where he lived two years, and being of an unsettled turn of mind he returned home to his Father with whom he stopped twelve months, he then went to service and staid till he attained the age of twenty or thereabouts, when he returned to Blackthorn where his Friends was then living; after residing there a short time he married a girl in that neighbourhood, but did not enjoy the matrimonial state but a short time.

On the 20th of December he was committed to Oxford Castle, on suspicion of killing, with intent to steal it, at the Hamlet of Blackthorn, one ewe sheep, the property of a Farmer of Blackthorn, but no bill being found against him he was discharged.

On the 13th of March, four days after his discharge from Oxford Castle) he called at the house of Mrs. Elizabeth York, a near neighbour, an old gentlewoman living at Shabbington Wood, with whom he spent some time in friendly conversation, but not having the fear of God before his eyes, he being moved and seduced by the instigation of the Devil, feloniously, willfully, maliciously, and with malice did make an assault on her, and with a certain knife and bar of the door, then and there did cut and strike divers mortal wounds upon the head and throat, of which she died; and also at the same time and place he did assault and grievously stab, maim, and wound, with intent to murder Elizabeth Hawes, spinster, in the head, face, and neck, and left her for dead; he then went up stairs to look for

plunder, but soon coming down he missed the girl that he had left for dead, he went directly in pursuit of her but could not find her; he then made off with haste; the girl having providentialy strength enough to go a short distance to alarm the neighbours who directly repaired to Mrs. York's house, where they found her with her head nearly severed from her body; they then went in pursuit of the Prisoner and took him at his Father's house, up the chimney, he was committed the next day to the County Goal at Aylesbury to await his trial.

During his confinement in the Gaol he appeared unconcerned, and his behaviour and expressions showed him to be very ignorant, and many of such expressions that was much unbecoming his situation.

He was taken from Aylesbury in order to take his trial at the Assizes to be held at Buckingham on the 29th of July, to which place he was conveyed on Tuesday, and on the Wednesday following came on his Trial, but the charge being read against him, he pleaded not guilty; the evidence appearing so clear against him, he was cast, and received sentence of Death, from Sir Vicary Gibbs, then Judge; who after admonishing him in the most pathetic manner, and to lose no time to make his peace with God. He was ordered to be executed on Friday.

From the time of his condemnation his conduct appeared blended with ignorance and sullenness, shewing no sign of repentance to the very last moment of his life. Thus ending his days in the prime of youth, being only 22 years of age.

He ascended the fatal Platform at half-past 9 o'Clock. After hanging the usual time, his body was cut down, and delivered to the surgeons for dissection.

W. Woodman, Printer, Aylesbury.

Handbill relating to the crime of Thomas Raisin.

brought before the Coroner two days later and was committed to Aylesbury Gaol.

Whilst awaiting trial at the Assizes, Reason candidly confessed that had he found the boy he would have killed him and when he discovered that Elizabeth Hawes had escaped he went after her with the fullest intention of shooting her with a gun that he had taken from the house.

On 31st July Reason appeared at Buckingham and although he pleaded 'Not Guilty', the evidence was so abundantly clear that he was found guilty in short order and sentenced to death – the judge, Sir Vicary Gibbs, advising him to make his peace with God as there could be no hope of a reprieve.

Two days later in front of a large crowd, Reason was hung outside the Town Hall at Aylesbury. His body was later removed for dissection.

The MONSTER of DAGNALL

Dagnall

Glance at a map of Buckinghamshire and half-way up and in the east of the county you will observe that it appears to jut into the adjoining shires like a broad thumb. Look more closely and you will see the tiny village of Dagnall at the very end of this thumb, straddling the modern A4146 as it threads its way from Leighton Buzzard to Hemel Hempstead. Passing from one county to another the road climbs slightly from Leighton Buzzard to Billington and leaving Bedfordshire meanders through Edlesborough and Dagnall to briefly pass through Bedfordshire again at Studham before entering Hertfordshire near Water End and Hemel Hempstead.

For thirty years John Payne of Billington set off at 3am on Thursday morning with his horse and cart, taking corn from the farmers to sell at the market at Hemel Hempstead, a dozen or so miles away. Any money he received he carefully placed in his pocket books, put them in his coat pocket and made his way

The Red Lion at Dagnall, as it stands now.

back home. If he fell asleep, his horse would slowly walk on, as he knew the way just as well as his master. Most evenings as he returned, Payne would stop at the Red Lion at Dagnall, climb down and have a few drinks with the customers, exchanging news and gossip with them. Although Payne might listen patiently to what the villagers told him it would usually be of humdrum matters, whilst he brought in news of the outside world, of the goings on in the market towns of Leighton Buzzard and Hemel Hempstead and no doubt of more important things, for these were momentous years in which they lived. There had been a revolution in France and the attendant 'Terror', followed by the ascendancy of the French nation under the leadership of Napoleon Bonaparte, who led her armies across Europe and whose navy threatened this country as Napoleon's legions gathered at Boulogne, no doubt talked about in the same way as the Battle of Britain would be discussed over a pint of beer a hundred and twenty-five years later.

Seldom could the villagers match Payne as the rural year unfolded with almost monotonous regularity. But in February 1815 the customers of the Red Lion certainly had a tale to tell, for a wicked murder had been committed in their village. Mrs Hall, who kept a shop, had been brutally done to death by some unknown assailant who had struck her about the head and had, for good measure, savagely cut her throat and then stolen her money. Her body had been found in a truly bloody state. The usual hue and cry had been made and one or two suspects were apprehended who had been seen in the vicinity of Mrs Hall's shop. Brought back for interrogation by the magistrate, they had to be released through lack of evidence. No one was convicted of the crime and although it would be repeated often enough the story began to lose its topicality. Payne would be warned to take care on the roads, as it was generally known that he often carried large amounts of money with him on his return from market. One can imagine him retorting, 'Just let them try!'

Some months later there would be news of the final battle of the Napoleonic Wars at Waterloo and peace and tranquility could return to this country.

Two years would pass until one evening when he called at the Red Lion he was informed of a most tragic accident that had occurred at Daniel Munn's farm. Munn rented a farm from the Earl of Bridgewater and had been married before, his first wife having died shortly after giving birth to a daughter. Munn had remarried and now his second wife had fallen down the well at their farm and drowned, leaving Munn to raise two children on his own. Payne knew Munn and his wife, for he used to call at their house to take poles and firewood from the farmer to sell and he could sympathise with him in his bereavement.

Almost six weeks later Munn saw Payne and arranged to meet him the following Thursday as he was passing through Dagnall to collect another load of firewood and poles from his premises and convey them to Billington.

At approximately 8.20pm on Thursday 1st May, Payne's cart drew up outside the Red Lion as usual. The horse waited patiently for his master to alight but there was no further movement. Some of the patrons of the pub, seeing the horse and cart arrive, waited for Payne to come bursting through the door and when, after a few minutes had elapsed he did not, they decided to go and rouse him from the stupor they assumed he had fallen into. They saw Payne's feet hanging over the foreboard of the cart but as they looked down at the recumbent figure they saw something that made them draw back in repugnance. Payne's throat had been but from ear to ear. The cart was awash with blood and the empty sacks were saturated with the sack carrier's gore. When they had overcome their initial shock they removed the body from the cart to the parlour of the Red Lion, laying it gently on the rough floor.

John Bennett, the landlord, sent for a local magistrate, the Reverend Horseman, who attended immediately. He made a cursory examination of the body, leaving it to Dr Steele of Berkhampstead to perform a thorough post-mortem examination. (Dr Steele would determine that not only had death been caused by a deep cut which had severed the carotid artery, the windpipe and the jugular vein, but Payne had also been stunned shortly beforehand by two blows to his head. Death had been almost instantaneous.) Mr Horseman had noticed however, that Payne's pocket books had been stolen and that such had been the force which the attacker had used to wrench them away from the sack carrier that his coat pocket had been torn completely off and was missing. (However, the murderer had missed the money that Payne had been carrying, for on this occasion he had put £43 in notes and 18 shillings in silver in another pocket.) As there were no professional Police to call upon, the Rev. Horseman, picking up a candle and lantern, now led the search for the perpetrator of such a vile crime. After walking back along the road for about three-quarters of a mile he found traces of blood which he followed to the place where he concluded the murder had been committed. He observed that there was a considerable amount of blood on the road and further, there was a deep indentation by the road-side where it seemed the cart had been drawn to one side near to a high hedge. Regarding the tracks, he also thought that at one stage the cart had been turned around. There was nothing else he could deduce from the scene of the crime and he returned to Dagnall. He wrote a letter outlining the circumstances of the slaying and, handing it to William Gurney, a farm labourer, directed him to take it to Dunstable, about five miles distant, and hand it over to the mail in order

The Dagnall–Hemel Hemspead Road where John Payne was fatally attacked – as it is now.

that it might reach the London Police. The Rev. Horseman now directed that a general search be made of the area and any suspicious rogues or likely suspects be apprehended and brought to him for interrogation.

The search for the murderer thus continued apace and one man, Daniel Rogers, was brought to the Red Lion, vehemently denying his involvement in the crime. William Gurney eventually returned from his errand to Dunstable and decided to carry on to work. He was employed by and lived with Daniel Munn, the tenant farmer who had lost his wife only a few weeks before. Gurney had been working at the farm the previous afternoon and had seen Munn leave the house. When he, Gurney, had gone for his tea he had found the door locked and had made his way to the Red Lion. After a few drinks he had walked home only to find the door still locked as Munn had not yet returned. He had then gone back to the Red Lion and had been caught up in the excitement of the night. As he approached the farmhouse this morning he saw Munn and called out to him, informing him of the murder. Gurney commenced work but after an hour broke off to have some breakfast at the house. He looked in the kitchen drawer where the butcher's knife that he used was kept but he could not find it. Gurney pondered this. He knew that Munn also used the knife for killing pigs but the last he had slaughtered had been a month before and Gurney had seen the knife only a few days previously. Somewhat bemused he ate his breakfast as best he could without it.

Munn meanwhile had walked down to the Red Lion and, mentioning to Bennett that it was a sad thing that his labourer had told him, asked to view the body. Bennett lit a candle and the two men entered the darkened room and stood either side of the corpse. Munn removed the sheet covering Payne and, looking firstly at the injuries that had been inflicted, then holding his hand, remarked how cold it felt. After a few minutes both men left the room. As they emerged from the parlour, Rogers, who was still detained 'under suspicion' called out, 'Munn! You can clear me. You know I met you last night at 8 o'clock and you had your brown frock rolled up!'

Munn looked at the prisoner and quickly said, 'Yes, I had my hands wrapped up in it.' He hurriedly left the inn and went back to his farm where Gurney saw him go to the barn and close and secure the door.

The stolid farm labourer went about his tasks during the course of the long day and in the early evening had to go to the barn to fetch a dung fork. He opened the door, entered and selected the tool. As he turned to leave he thought he saw a rat amongst the straw that lay on the floor and poked at it with the fork. He peered closely at the object and realised that it was not a rodent at all but a torn coat pocket! Gurney carefully considered the situation. He knew from the previous night that when Mr Horseman had examined Payne's coat he had noticed that a pocket had been torn off in the struggle between the murderer and his victim. Now here he was looking at a torn coat pocket. It was very queer. Very queer indeed. He decided to leave the pocket where it was; you did not know what folks might accuse you of if you suddenly turned up with a detached pocket which might have some connection with a murder, and left for the Red Lion, after consulting Daniel Munn's brother, who advised him to report the matter. Upon reaching the pub he recounted the odd tale to Bennett. The landlord wasted no time but accompanied by a party of customers made his way to the barn where Gurney showed them the pocket he had found.

Picking up the item, Bennett rummaged about in the straw and discovered a couple of pocket-books. There was also a note which someone recognised as being in Payne's handwriting. As the grim-faced men left the barn they met Munn who demanded, 'What have you got there?'

Bennett replied, 'Payne's pocket-books which I found in your barn!'

The farmer blanched but said nothing.

Bennett went on, 'You must go with me. I shall not let you go out of my sight till you go before a magistrate.' Taking hold of Munn's arm he led him off in the direction of the Red Lion.

As they made their way towards the village Bennett exclaimed, 'Good God! How could these books get into your barn?'

Munn made the rather lame excuse, 'I suppose it was some of those trampers.'

Bennett enquired, 'Did you see any trampers here?' Munn shook his head.

Bennett went on, 'There were some soldiers in your barn last Monday morning but they got away and went to Dunstable that night.'

Munn answered, 'I did not see them.'

Bennett declared that he had not seen any 'trampers' about that week adding, 'I feel it will go hard with you, these books being found there.'

Munn was forced to agree, 'Yes, I suppose it will.'

He was brought before the Reverend Horseman who carefully examined the farmer's clothes. He observed that the smock frock worn by Munn had been washed but on looking more closely he could discern some blood-stains especially on the sleeves and cuffs. 'Nosebleed,' explained Munn. Undeterred, Mr Horseman ordered that Munn's house be searched and in due course a blue coat was brought in. On the lining of one of the sleeves were found more bloodstains whilst the cuff had been cut off. Again Munn attempted to dismiss the discovery by saying that he suffered from frequent nosebleeds.

Mr Horseman continued his examination, but now scrutinising Munn's breeches. One of the knees appeared to be stained but this had been rubbed quite hard in an effort to hide the blotches. He next looked at Munn's stockings and seeing that these were stained with blood as well, he observed that there was no wound on Munn's legs that would account for these.

Mr Horseman turned to Munn and asked him to relate his movements on the day of the murder. Munn swore that he had been at home at the time of the murder but in this he was contradicted by several witnesses who had seen him loitering near the scene and then shortly afterwards had seen him running home with his hands wrapped up in his smock frock as if he was carrying something. Rogers, who had originally been arrested, 'on suspicion', now became a very valuable witness to Munn's activities of the night before.

The farmer was quickly committed and appeared before Mr Justice Dallas at Hertfordshire Assizes on the 24th July and after an all-day trial was found guilty. The Judge, in sentencing him to death the following Monday, exhorted him to seek repentence. On the eve of his execution, Munn was visited by the Chaplain who encouraged him to join him in prayers but the heretofore callous killer broke down and shocked the Chaplain by admitting that not only had he attacked and killed Payne but that he had murdered Mrs Hall two years before. He had gone to her shop early one morning and waiting for an opportunity to get behind her had struck her down, making sure she would not bear witness against him by cutting her throat with a similar knife to that which he had used on Payne. He had stolen £40 from her to pay off debts he had incurred from the Earl of Bridgewater and other people.

Nor was this all! He further confessed to the murder of his wife some weeks before attacking Payne. He had waited until she had turned her back on him, had crept up behind her and struck her with a billet of wood. She had been merely stunned and Munn had then dragged his wife to the well and shoved her down head first, killing her. They had quarrelled during their marriage but Munn hastily added that they had not had words on the day he had killed her.

The next day, before a large crowd, he urged the spectators to be warned by his fate before being hanged. It is thought that the villagers of Dagnall rested more easily afterwards.

A SWIFT and SUDDEN DEATH

Buckingham 1835

In its issue of 18th July, 1835, the Bucks Gazette startled its readers with the news that 'A recent diabolical and cruel murder late on Saturday night or early on Sunday morning last was committed on the body of Thomas Swift, an aged chimney sweep, a recipient pauper of the parish of Fringford, Oxford'.

Thomas, who was in his 96th year – a truly great age for the times – lived with his son, James, and his family in Gawcott Road, Buckingham. He apparently slept in the outhouse on a 'miserable bed or rather a bedstead'. Whether this was because James had a large family and this was the only place for the old man to sleep or he had become too cantankerous in his old age to have in the house we are not told.

On Saturday, 11th July Thomas retired to his 'miserable bed'. The next morning it was discovered that he had been brutally done to death. There were three distinct wounds to his head resulting in a fractured skill and his right arm was smashed, presumably when he had feebly tried to ward off the blows rained down on him by his assailant.

Now, there are and always have been certain procedures that should be carried out upon the discovery of a murder. First and foremost the Police must be notified, then usually a doctor is summoned to examine the body and pronounce life extinct. The Swift family, however, decided to do none of these. Removing all the bedsheets and the old man's shirt and nightcap which, as can be imagined, were all very bloodied, they placed a cap on his head, wrapped his body up in a blanket and pinned up his chin before calling in an old woman to 'lay out' the body. What she thought as she went about her task is difficult to imagine, working in a place, the walls and floor of which were smattered with blood and brains. When she had finished, she placed a sheet over the corpse and left. She said after that she had seen nothing amiss and it can only be conjectured that she must have been extremely short-sighted and it may have been for that reason that she had been chosen by the Swifts. They meantime had hastily called on the sexton to toll the Church bell for the late lamented Thomas.

If the Swifts were hoping to have old Thomas buried before any enquiries could be made into his sudden exit from t his world, they were singularly mistaken. These things have a habit of becoming known, especially in a small town and in the early nineteenth century Buckingham was a tiny and to some extent remote borough. Before long, word of the demise of the ancient chimney sweep had reached the ear of the authorities who decided to take a hand in the matter and postponed the hurriedly arranged funeral and arranged for a post-mortem examination instead.

The autopsy was duly carried out and the surgeon said that in his opinion the old man had been murdered, as his injuries could not have been caused by a fall even from a miserable bed.

At the Inquest James Swift and one of his sons, also named Thomas, were intensively examined by the Coroner but to no firm conclusion, as after a ten hour enquiry, the jury returned saying that Thomas had been murdered by some person or persons unknown.

This was a most unsatisfactory state of affairs and obviously, despite the Inquest verdict, the gravest suspicion attached itself to the son and grandson, especially as by now a bloodstained hammer had been found under the bed upon which the aged sweep had been murdered and it was proved to belong to a member of the Swift family.

On the day of the funeral the two main suspects were regarded with intense interest. James, it was later reported, 'trembled in every limb but shed no tears'.

There was a general unease about Buckingham, firstly because the perpetrators of such a brutal murder had not been apprehended and secondly because there appeared to be a general reluctance on the part of the authorities to pursue the investigation. Bear in mind that there were, at this time, no professional Police in the town.

However, a few days later came the dramatic news that the grandson, Thomas, had admitted killing his grandfather. He was brought before the examining magistrate and made a long

The Old Gaol at Buckingham where the murderer of old Thomas Swift was lodged.

rambling confession.

'I sat up in bed. It seemed as if there were serpents all about me . . . I though they were very pretty, I felt so light. I felt as if I was a spirit . . . they told me I must make away with somebody, that I must kill three people . . . they gave me the hammer and took me into the shop and I went in to where my grandfather was. I felt for his head. I lifted up the hammer and hit him three times, then it seemed to me I had not done for him so I took up a piece of wood and hit him. I went to bed pleased with what I had done. I lay down very contentedly and went to sleep.'

Thomas Swift was committed for trial for the murder of his grandfather and as he left the dock became so violent that it took six men to remove him.

At the Buckinghamshire Assizes it could be seen that he was suffering under a strong mental delusion and he was duly committed to be detained during his Majesty's pleasure.

A SUMMER MADNESS

Denham 1870

There can be few more pleasant villages in South Bucks than Denham. Separated as it is from the metropolitan sprawl of Uxbridge by only a few fields, it nevertheless offers an oasis of tranquility. With its ancient church and old houses lining the main street and the gently flowing stream nearby combining to effect an air of calmness seldom now found in this modern hectic world of ours, it is very easy to imagine that it has lain dormant for several centuries, slumbering peacefully through the years.

Yet it was in Denham in 1870 that virtually a whole family was massacred in Cheapside Lane. This event, so terrible a stain upon such a village, should, one would suppose, be enough butchery for any place but just sixteen years later another murder was to take place reviving memories of the earlier killings.

Thursday 26th August, 1886 was one of the hottest days of the year. The temperature was described as 'excessive' by one local newspaper and had reached an astonishing 118 degrees! (Actually, it was the report in the newspaper that was 'excessive' as the Meteorological Office had recorded the temperature as rising to a mere 86 degrees!) Nevertheless, for the men and women who laboured all day in the fields in such sweltering weather, it must have been nigh unbearable.

Two men, employed by James Moreton of Denham Court, were hoeing turnips in these stifling conditions. One was forty-six year old Charles Plumridge working alongside Alfred Hitch, a former soldier who had served abroad in far hotter climates. In the next field to them laboured Lydia Giles, busy gleaning. At mid-day she glanced up and observed Hitch, who had been lodging with her, walk slowly past. He stopped and showed her a florin which he explained that Mr Moreton had given him as a sub. He added that he was now going into the village to purchase some beer. For a moment or two she

The Dog and Duck Public House, Uxbridge Road, Denham, where the murderer drew attention to himself – as it stands today.

watched as he wandered off before resuming her task. Lydia's son, Joseph, was somewhat surprised when Hitch walked into the house, removed his smock and donned his jacket. He showed the two shilling piece to Joseph and invited him to go for a drink. Needing no second bidding he accompanied the lodger to the Falcon public house where they drank their beer. However, after slaking his thirst, Giles declined the offer of further drink, made his excuses and left.

Hitch also left and walked to the Uxbridge Road, dropping in at the Dog and Duck just outside the town. Calling for a pint of beer from the landlord, Henry Woodley, Hitch sat down. He had consumed only some of the beer when he requested another which Woodley supplied him and for which Hitch paid with half a sovereign. The landlord kept his eye on Hitch for he seemed to be acting in a somewhat peculiar way. He lifted the pot of beer up but did not drink from it and instead dropped it on the floor, breaking it. Apologising, he paid for the breakage and resumed his seat. Suddenly he jumped up and shrieked, 'Look! There the bugger is. Look at him pulling that wire!'

A hush fell upon the regulars of the public house as they

starred at Hitch. Woodley leant across the bar and bellowed, 'Sit down, you mad wretch.'

But Hitch now looked under the bench, exclaiming, 'Look! Look at him!' He glanced up and met the stern eye of the landlord and slowly sat down. Peace seemed to settle on the pub and the customers started to resume their talk, when suddenly, after a few minutes Hitch cried out, 'I've murdered one man today! Charley Plumridge!'

Everyone's head turned towards Hitch as he made his astounding claim. Wild-eyed he turned to Woodley and demanded more beer but the landlord had had quite enough of Hitch and his hysterical outbursts and refused to serve him.

'I've plenty of money,' he sneered but Woodley was adamant and showed him the door. Grumbling, Hitch shuffled off in the direction of Uxbridge.

Whilst this astonishing behaviour was going on another of Moreton's employees was rather surprised to see, as he was working in the fields, a basket, a bottle containing tea and a handkerchief wrapped around some food floating slowly down the stream. Mystified, he retrieved these items and pondered on its meaning.

Two days later, William Peterill, a gamekeeper, was out on

Old Denham Village.

his rounds when, walking through a covert he noticed a man lying on his back with his jacket across his head. He assumed that the man was having a quick forty winks and Peterill approached him cautiously and enquired softly, 'Are you having a rest mate?' Receiving no response he edged closer. There did not appear to be a flicker of movement from the recumbent figure and Peterill, his curiosity aroused reached down and gently lifted the jacket from the body. What he saw made him recoil in horror for the man was not asleep but dead with his head battered to a pulp! The shocked gamekeeper was transfixed for several moments as he stared down at the sight that lay before him. Then he gently lay the jacket back across the body and ran as fast as he could to Denham Court where he gasped out his story to Mr Moreton.

Peterill led a party of men back to the covert and showed them the body. One of the men recognised the victim as Charles Plumridge, who lived alone and because of this had not been missed for the past two days. As gently as they could the men lifted the body up and carried it to the Swan public house in the village where a post-mortem examination would take place.

The Police were then informed and Inspector Sapwell took immediate charge of the case directing his men to make diligent enquiries in the neighbourhood in an effort to trace the murderer. It was as a result of these 'diligent enquiries' that the strange conduct of Alfred Hitch came to light. Hitch was not unknown to the forces of law and order for he had come to their attention on previous occasions for attempting to commit suicide for which he had appeared before the Court for punishment. All the endeavours of the Buckinghamshire Constabulary were now concentrated upon their prime suspect who had apparently disappeared into thin air.

The Coroner for South Bucks opened the Inquest at the Swan and had heard several witnesses when the dramatic news was received that Hitch had been apprehended. His mother lived in the Basingstoke area so that when the Hampshire Police had discovered a man wandering around in the vicinity of her house they had promptly detained him on suspicion and had delivered him over to their Buckinghamshire colleagues. Hitch attended the remainder of the Inquest. The reporters who were also present were able to describe the prisoner much more freely than their modern-day counterparts would be allowed to. They recounted that he was about thirty-five years of age and had served with the Army in India where he had been found guilty at a Court Martial of gross insubordination and of making a murderous attack upon an officer and had been sentenced to seven years imprisonment for which he had been returned to England to serve. He had been branded, they reported, with the letters B C on the inside of his left arm. This stood for 'Bad Character' and had been put there on his discharge from the Army. (With all this coverage in the newspapers, one wonders how he could ever hope for a fair trial.) A verdict of wilful murder was returned by the Coroner's Jury and he was committed for trial.

When he therefore appeared at Bedfordshire Assizes much was made of his mental state and his suicide attempts. The Jury, although finding him guilty as charged added a strong recommendation to mercy. Hitch, in reply to the Judge's sentence of death replied that he had no recollection of the crime.

Shortly before he was due to be hanged it was announced that Hitch had been granted a reprieve by the Home Secretary.

GET CARTER !!

Slough 1882

On a cold Sunday in late January, 1882, the sturdy figure of Police Sergeant Hebbes could be seen slowly making his way through the rain along William Street, Slough. As he approached the Somerset Arms, he could hear the sound of men's voices issuing from the dimly lit beerhouse. Hebbes paused and peered in. He could see several men enjoying their ale, most of whom he knew. He noticed, in particular, those standing at the bar. Among them was Francis Carter, a canalman who had once worked on the Slough brickfields, and Tom Long, who was also known as Brummy. Joseph Piner, the landlord, seeing Hebbes and realising that it was now ten o'clock called 'Time' and started to clear away the men's glasses and usher the drinkers out of his beerhouse. As the men came out onto the street they noticed the Police Sergeant and, wishing him good-night made their separate ways home.

Carter, who lived in nearby Pressfield Place, was accompanied by Long who lodged with him. Hebbes watched

William Street, Slough.

The Somerset Arms – where Carter drank before he was murdered.

the men until they were swallowed up in the gloom before resuming his patrol. He little realised that he would see both Carter and Long under vastly different circumstances next day.

Carter had been drinking at the Somerset Arms since Piner had re-opened its doors at 6pm that evening. Indeed, he had also been there when it had opened around mid-day, only leaving when it had closed some two hours or so later and he had returned home for his dinner, taking with him some beer to consume there. Now, as he staggered home, he was fairly drunk; Long, on the other hand was quite sober. Mary Ann Carter had prepared supper for her husband and Long and when the two men came in, they, Mary Ann and two of her five children sat down at the table.

Carter, however, was not hungry and after a few minutes stood up and announced that he was going out. He sent Mary Ann upstairs for a sack and when she asked him where he was going he gruffly replied that it was no business of hers. However, as he left he did say that he was going to shift his nephew's tools which were at Little's brickfields. Mrs Carter listened as she heard her husband walk along the passageway into the road, then sat down to await his return as he had ordered her to do.

At 7am the next day, Monday 30th January, Charles Reed made his way across the brickfields near the Railway Station. As he reached the place where he was to work, he saw the body of a man lying on its side. Looking closely he recognised it as that of Francis Carter. Reed called out to another brickworker, Frank Clayton, 'Frank! Here's a man. Here's a navvy!' Both men now looked down at the still figure. Seeing a sack by the body they picked it up and replaced the tools they found by it back in the place where they had been hidden by other brickmen when they had finished their work the previous Saturday. Reed and Clayton then went to report their discovery at the Police Station.

They returned with the formidable Sergeant Hebbes. He looked over the body, satisfied himself that there was no sign of life, then cast an eye over the surrounding area. He noticed that there were four sets of footprints. Two sets belonged to Reed and Clayton, the third were those of Carter but the fourth set? Who did they belong to?

Hebbes also looked through the pockets of Carter's jacket, but found no money in them.

Other people now arrived at the scene either in connection with the investigation or just merely out of idle curiosity. By so doing they obliterated the footprints discovered by the Police Sergeant.

Among those who attended in an official capacity were Superintendent Dunham and Dr Buee.

The doctor made an initial examination of the body. He observed that Carter had been dealt several blows to the back of his head which had been inflicted by a heavy blunt instrument, causing the skull to fracture and leaving blood and parts of the scalp lying on the ground. There were, Dr Buee concluded from a later post mortem examination, no other marks of violence.

Dunham and Hebbes now began their enquiries and immediately visited Carter's home and closely interviewed Mary Ann. (She had been acquainted with her husband's death by Frank Clayton before the arrival of the Police Officers.) Later that day the two Policemen went to Windsor where they saw Tom Long who was working as a coal heaver. 'Do you know your landlord's been murdered?', the Superintendent bluntly asked.

'Yes,' replied Long giving the name of the man who had informed him.

'When did you last see him?', Dunham enquired.

'I was drinking with him at Piner's house until shutting up time,' was the response.

Dunham now wanted to know where they had gone after the beerhouse had closed.

Long explained, 'We both went home and I and the missus and two children sat down and had some supper.'

'What became of Carter?'

'He would not have any supper,' Long replied, 'but sent the missus upstairs for a sack and wanted me to go out with him. I told him I would not go and went down to the privy. When I came back I saw him going out with a sack rolled up under his arm.'

It was at this point that Superintendent Dunham decided to arrest Long on suspicion of murder. Long asked if he could fetch his coat as they prepared to leave. On their arrival at Slough Police Station Dunham took the coat and examined it. He found some brick-earth on the left elbow and on part of the skirt of the coat which he would assert was identical in colour to that found in the brickfield where the body of Carter had been discovered. On the side of the coat was a pocket in which, Dunham deduced, an implement with earth on it had been secreted recently as there was still some earth remaining on the lining.

Dunham, also looked over the sack which had been found by Carter's body and formed the opinion that the marks on it were footprints in mud identical to the earth on Long's coat. (The footprints could not have been all that clear as at no time did Dunham suggest that they were identical to those worn by the prisoner.)

On the Tuesday following the murder the Inquest was opened at the North Star public house in William Street. The evidence of the finding of Carter's body was given, as was the result of Dr Buee's post mortem examination. Sergeant Hebbes then told of finding the sets of footprints but had to admit that he had been unable to preserve them owing to the numbers of persons milling about at the scene. However, he was able to say that when he had seen the prisoner at the Somerset Arms on Sunday night, Long had been wearing the coat which was exactly similar to the one now produced in Court; the one Long had worn at the time of his arrest and on which the brick-earth had been found.

After Superintendent Dunham had recounted his investigations leading up to the arrest of Long, the Coroner adjourned the Inquest for a week and on its resumption it was held at the more respectable surroundings of the Police Station.

Mary Ann Carter was first to give evidence. Tearfully she told of how she had waited for her husband to come back from his drinking at the Somerset Arms. How he had arrived with Tom Long just after 10pm slightly the worse for wear and how they had all sat down for supper although her husband had not eaten anything. He had then asked her to fetch a sack from upstairs and announced that he was going out and had instructed her to wait up for him. This she had done until after midnight, adding that Long had gone to bed shortly after her husband had left on his nocturnal errand. Mary Ann was adamant that Long could not have gone out without her knowledge, all that she would say was that whilst she was upstairs fetching the sack for her husband Long could have gone out to the closet and been back before she had returned.

Mrs Carter was then asked if her husband usually went out at night and she replied that he was 'Not in the habit of staying out all night'. Later she admitted that when he had worked in the brickfields he had stayed out as late as 10 or 12 o'clock when he had been burning bricks in the kiln. She added that he had been out all night on occasions but not within the past six months, of that she was certain.

Resuming her narrative Mrs Carter continued that she had remained downstairs until she became too cold and had then gone to her bedroom which she shared with her five children. She maintained that she was awake all night and she was sure that Long had not left the house at all until early the next morning when he had arisen to go to work. When she heard him moving about she had asked him what time it was and he replied that he had 'heard the clock strike five and supposed it was now something to six'.

Mrs Carter was then questioned about a quarrel between her husband and Tom Long when he had lodged with them before. She replied that a fight had taken place when her husband thought that Long had been paying too much attention to her. Afterwards Long had left their house but had returned to lodge with them when the Carters had moved into Pressfield Place. This had occurred some eighteen months before and they had not argued since.

Sarah, one of the five Carter children, was next to give evidence. She had heard her father going up the passage and had also heard Long going to bed in the room next to where she lay. She was also shown the coat produced at the Inquest and identified it as the one Long had worn on Sunday night.

Joseph Pizzey, Carter's nephew, was then called. He stated that he had no quarrel with the deceased and had no idea why Carter had wanted to move his tools. He had lodged with the Carters for a time but he was of the opinion that they were not a happy couple as Carter was very jealous of his wife and had heard them quarrelling on more than one occasion. Pizzey was questioned further about this and added that he had heard Carter mention that he believed that Long had 'a little to do with his missus'. However, Pizzey was quick to assure the Inquest that he himself had never seen any impropriety take place between his landlady and Long.

Thomas Mould who had also lodged with the Carters mentioned that if Carter and Long quarrelled, Mrs Carter always took Long's part and another thing he had noticed was that whereas Mrs Carter always referred to him (Mould) as 'lodger Tom', she always called Long, 'Tom'. One can imagine the knowing looks that passed among the members of the public present when these little gems of indiscretions were disclosed. Mould added that when he and Carter were working on the canal, Carter had talked about his wife, Mary Ann and Long and had muttered that he would have an 'alteration'.

Another witness averred that Carter had told him that since Long had returned to lodge with them he had 'started up the same old game'.

The Coroner's Jury then retired and on their return announced, somewhat ominously for the Police that Carter had been murdered by some person or persons unknown; not the prisoner, let it be noted.

Long was now brought up before the Magistrates for the committal proceedings to take place. Once again the evidence which had been heard at the Inquest was gone into. In addition Superintendent Dunham stated that when he had removed Long's shoes at Slough Police Station he had noticed earth adhering to the soles. When asked to account for this Long had replied that sometime between 9 and 10am on Sunday morning he had walked across the field to where Carter had been picking some greens.

The Police brought along one witness who said that on Sunday morning he had engaged Long to come and cut his hair and another who said that he had seen Long coming from Carter's house and go to the house where he was to cut hair but did not see him cross any field to speak to Carter.

At the end of the proceedings the Chairman of the bench asked Dunham if he had any further evidence. The Superintendent could only add that it was his opinion that earth could not cling to the prisoner's boots from Sunday morning as it had been too dry, whereas it had rained on Sunday night and earth could have stuck to Long's boots if he had walked across the brickfields. He had to admit that he was unable to produce the chopper which had been in general use at the Carter house, which Dunham suspected had been used to commit the murder and which had not been seen since the killing. Dunham argued that if Long had gone out to the back of the house he would pass the place where it was usually kept. The Superintendent had also walked the distance from Carter's house to where his body had been discovered and it had only taken him seven minutes to cover the ground between.

The Chairman of the Magistrates then said that the evidence brought before them was insufficient to commit the prisoner for trial and he would therefore be released. At the same time, he warned, if there was any fresh evidence found he could be rearrested.

Long walked from the Court and was immediately treated to drinks by some well-wishers after which, it was reported, he went to a barber's for a close shave, presumably the second he had had that day.

The murder of Francis Carter remained unsolved and the question is, had the Police arrested the wrong man or, had they apprehended the murderer but were not in a position to prove it conclusively? Superintendent Dunham was convinced that he had the right man. He believed that Long had the motive, either the quarrel between himself and Carter over the attention allegedly paid by the lodger to Mrs Carter and which apparently surfaced each time Carter drank or, Dunham reasoned, there was some substance to Carter's allegation and Long had been paying attention to Mary Ann and wanted his landlord out of the way, seeing his opportunity to murder Carter when he went out on Sunday night. Dunham calculated that it would take just seven minutes to go from Pressfield Place to where Carter was murdered. Not a great length of time for Long to be absent from the house but he would have to rely totally on Mrs Carter saying that her lodger did not leave the house that night.

Was it coincidence that the chopper which had been used at the Carter household by several people including the lodgers until just before the murder could not be found afterwards by the Police? Had Long taken it with him, killed Carter and disposed of it afterwards? Dunham stated that when he examined Long's coat, he found an inside pocket which could have been used to carry such a weapon. Long had the opportunity of disposing of it on Monday morning by throwing it in the River Thames, for he worked at the nearby Railway Station. Dunham also said that there was earth on the sleeve and skirt of Long's coat as well as on his shoes which Long explained had got there when he went looking for Carter on Sunday morning. Dunham produced a witness who said Long did not go across the fields to see Carter. Even if he had, Dunham thought, would a man get earth on his coat just talking to someone? Would it be more likely that it got there during the fatal struggle?

It was most unfortunate that Sergeant Hebbes either did not, or could not preserve the bootprints found at the scene to see if they resembled those of Thomas Long's footwear. (It is to Hebbes' credit that he did not, in an effort to bolster the case against Long, suggest at any time that the fourth set of bootprints were similar to those on the soles of the footwear worn by the prisoner.)

Or were the Police completely wrong? Had Carter encountered someone who took exception to his presence in the brickfields that night, possibly one of the brickworkers whose tools he was 'moving' and who decided to teach him a lesson, albeit a fatal one?

William Street, Slough – where the victim lived – taken a few years after.

MURDER at the PHEASANT

Lent Green, Burnham 1905

For almost four years, Henry Charles Taylor or Boy King as he liked to be called, the son of the landlord of the Pheasant public house at Lent Green, had been keeping company with Lillian Anne Baker, a domestic servant and the youngest daughter of a retired Policeman and his wife. Annie, as she was known, lived with her parents a short distance away from the Pheasant at 'Eastview' in Lent Rise.

They were going to be married at Christmas 1905 and live with Boy King's sister and brother-in-law, Mr and Mrs Frederick Cock, until they got a house and Annie and Mrs Cock were going into partnership as dressmakers. However, Mr Baker was not overkeen on the match as he thought that Taylor, who worked as a carman, had no real prospects in life.

The 'happy' couple had had their little arguments too. Annie had chided Boy King about his habit of frequenting public houses. She had been embarrassed recently when he had been

High Street, Burnham.

39

summoned to appear before Beaconsfield Police Court for causing an obstruction with his horse and cart which he had left unattended in the street whilst inside a local pub. (His next appearance at the same Court would be on a far more serious charge.)

On the other hand Boy King was upset by Annie flirting with other men and when he had mentioned it to her she had promised not to do so in the future. The fact that Taylor had a withered leg may have preyed on his mind somewhat in this respect.

It may be that the initial passion that Annie had felt for Boy King was waning, for she had confided to her father that although she liked Taylor she thought she could not marry him. If Annie was trifling with a young man's affections she was treading on very dangerous ground.

On the afternoon of Saturday, 28th October, Taylor had been with the local football team to see them play at Cookham. On his return he had met Annie and they had passed Fred Cock on the road leading to Lent Rise. They were quietly talking to each other. They had then gone their separate ways home. A little while later, Annie left Eastview with a couple of empty bottles and walked the few yards to the Pheasant. Again Boy King and Annie were seen together for a short time and then they disappeared from sight.

Just before 10 o'clock Taylor re-entered the Pheasant and appeared somewhat agitated. He ordered some beer and cigars and treated several of those about him. Taylor sought out his sister and handing her a ring exclaimed, 'Goodbye Flo, you won't see me any more. I've killed Annie! Keep this ring as I won't need it.'

Taylor next spoke to his brother-in-law and offered him his watch. 'Keep it till I want it again,' he told the astonished man.

No one appeared to believe what Taylor had said, so did not make the effort to go and look and see just what had happened to his fiancée, but if this seemed rather extraordinary what took place next was even more so. For as the pub closed, the family sat down and ate supper, during the course of which Taylor kept repeating to his sister, 'If you come Flo, I'll show you where Annie lays.' It could hardly have been one of the

The Pheasant at Lent Green – where 'Boy King' murdered his fianceé – as it stands today.

happiest of meals for Taylor then broke down and cried. It began to dawn on Fred Cock that something was wrong and eventually he offered to go outside with Taylor to see what had happened.

Taylor agreed to this as long as Flo went too. He then took his sister, brother-in-law and father to the garden at the rear of the Pheasant and, pointing, cried out, 'There, can't you see?'

Cock, peering into the gloom, replied, 'No.' Taylor asked him once more and Cock struck a match and the party saw the body of Annie Baker lying quite still in the cabbage patch. Flo screamed and her husband took her back inside the pub followed by Taylor and his father. 'Look after her Fred,' he told his son-in-law, 'while I go across to Burnham to fetch the Police.'

After Taylor senior had gone, Fred Cock turned to his brother-in-law and asked, 'Well, Boy King what did you do it for?'

'She asked me to do it,' he responded. 'She asked me to kiss her good-bye and she asked me to do it.'

A doctor from Burnham attended and after a quick

examination stated that Annie was indeed dead and gave his opinion that she had been strangled. This was confirmed later after a post-mortem examination.

The Police, in the shape of Sergeant Heath and Police Constable Milner, were next to arrive on the scene. As soon as he saw them, Taylor blurted out, 'I've done it! I've done it! It was her wish that I should do it. When are you going to take me away?'

Taylor then asked the Sergeant if he could see Annie once more. Heath agreed to this request and, accompanied by P.C.Milner, Taylor returned to where the body of his fiancée lay. He knelt down and kissed her several times before standing up and whispering, 'Good-by my gal.' He looked into Milner's face and sighed, 'She's happy now.'

Sergeant Heath informed Taylor that he would be arrested to which he replied, 'Yes I done it. I strangled her. She asked me to do it and it was her wish to die. Is she dead Mr Heath?'

The Police Sergeant nodded and Taylor added, 'She is dead. I shall die too. Does her people know yet?'

Heath took his prisoner to Beaconsfield Police Station where Inspector Marks charged him with the murder and examined him. He noticed that Taylor had scratches on his left wrist and blood on his jacket.

Taylor was swiftly committed by the Beaconsfield Magistrates, before whom he had so recently appeared, to the Buckinghamshire Assizes.

When he stood trial, Taylor's mental state was enquired into. Two medical officers testified that he was of low intelligence and that when he consumed alcohol he was scarcely responsible for his actions and that he had, on the night in question, acted under an 'uncontrollable impulse'.

The Jury found him guilty of murder but added a recommendation to mercy. In sentencing him to death, the Judge informed Taylor that he would pass that recommendation onto the Home Office, adding that he had tried no sadder case.

Shortly before the date set for Taylor's execution it was announced that he had been reprieved.

A Rural Tragedy

Great Horwood 1906

As Good Friday 1906 dawned over Great Horwood, men and women bestirred themselves and made ready for the day's labours, which for some of them consisted of working on the farms surrounding one of the most picturesque of North Buckinghamshire villages. No doubt many of those who thought about it at all realised that this day was one of the holiest days in the Church calendar. How many also gave thought to the fact that it was also Friday 13th?

Amos King lived with his wife, Eliza Jane, and their adopted son Fred and two other children, boarded out to them by a charitable institution, in a cottage in School Lane next to the Church of St. James. Their cottage adjoined that of one Thomas Hurst. Amos, having arisen shortly before 6am and having been assured by his wife that Fred was getting ready to go to Winslow, left for work on a nearby farm.

Mrs King busied herself about the cottage, only to be

Great Horwood at the turn of the century.

interrupted by a knock at the front door as the baker, Joseph Hanson, called just before 7am making his way round the village. After a short conversation Mr Hanson sold Mrs King sixpence worth of hot cross buns and went on his way.

A few minutes later several people heard the sound of a gunshot, but assuming it was someone scaring birds thought no more about it.

At 7.15am Amos, who was only working a hundred yards away from his cottage and who had also heard the shot returned home for his breakfast. As he entered by the back way he saw what he thought was a bundle lying in the doorway of Hurst's cottage. Amos approached, curious to see what the bundle was, and was horrified when he realised that it was the body of his wife. Desperately he called out her name but receiving no answer and fearing the worst he ran back to his employer Mr Sear and breathlessly informed him that something dreadful had happened to Eliza. Leaving the distraught man, Sear with several other of his labourers went directly to the cottages to ascertain for themselves what had taken place. They were confronted by the same terrible sight that had greeted Amos King. Eliza lay quite dead, partly outside Hurst's cottage, with a large gaping wound to her breast. She had evidently been killed by a gun which had been fired by someone who had been standing very close to her.

Cautiously Sear peered over the corpse of Mrs King and into the cottage. What he saw next must have tested his nerve to the utmost, for inside lay the body of Albert King, Amos' brother, with a large wound to his throat and the door, walls and floor of the cottage were covered in blood. As he took in the ghastly sight, Sear noticed that Albert clasped a razor in his right hand, whilst in a corner of the room stood a converted rifle.

Dr Mobberley of Winslow was urgently summoned and after a brief examination directed the body of Mrs King to be taken indoors and laid beside that of her brother-in-law.

Sergeant Wootton of the Winslow Police, who had attended at the same time, swiftly conducted his enquiries into the matter and by Saturday the Inquest was able to be held in the school.

St. James' Church, Great Horwood – as people prepared to go to church they heard of the terrible events that had taken place nearby.

Tudor Cottage, Great Horwood – where a double tragedy unfolded on Good Friday 1906.

The Swan, Great Horwood – the murderer had his last drink here.

Amos King, after telling how he had found the body of his wife, went on to say that both he and Eliza had remonstrated with his brother on several occasions about his drinking, in fact only a day or two before the tragedy he had fetched him out of the Six Lords public house at nearby Singleborough. Albert's only response to their continual fussing was that they had no call to trouble him, it was all his own fault and no-one else's. To try and help out, Eliza had gone to Albert's cottage at Singleborough two or three times a week to clean up. Amos had last seen his brother on Thursday morning and knew that he had been staying at his neighbour's cottage on that and several nights previously, although his cottage at Singleborough was quite comfortable. Hurst and Albert were frequent drinkers together and Amos knew that Albert had been drinking at the Swan at Great Horwood on Thursday night before coming back to Hurst's where he heard them talking until 3am. Almost as an aside he admitted that his brother had attempted to commit suicide some years before but had been alright since then, except that he would drink.

There was a slight stir in the schoolroom as Amos finished giving his evidence and Thomas Hurst was called. He was most emphatic that he had slept alone in his cottage on Thursday night and that there had been no-one else with him. He had seen Albert in the Six Lords about 8 o'clock that night but he had left and come straight home at 10 o'clock. Hurst admitted that Albert often visited him and had on occasions stopped all night; he even conceded that Albert had stayed with him on Wednesday but he was adamant that if his neighbour had said he was there on Thursday night it just was not true. He might have been talking to himself as he often did when he had had a drop and, he added, he had had plenty to drink on Thursday.

On the morning of the tragedy he had got up and left his home at 6am, noticing Amos on his way to work. He could not remember if he had fastened his back door on leaving. He had then gone for a walk as far as the Lone Tree Inn (now on the main Bletchley–Buckingham road) where he had a drink and heard of the incident at Great Horwood. His reaction was one of surprise but he had not returned to his cottage, instead he had gone for another walk and had another pint. He was upset about what had happened because Albert had been a great friend of his.

Superintendent Lait for the Police questioned him about the statement he had just made and Hurst admitted going to the Six Lords at 5 o'clock on Thursday afternoon, then leaving and sleeping alone in his cottage with his clothes on. Albert, he conceded, might have gone into his cottage after he had left for his walk on Good Friday morning.

In reply to a Juror's request, Hurst now acknowledged that he had met Albert at the Crown public house in Great Horwood about 4 o'clock on Thursday afternoon before they went off to the Six Lords. He had left and gone to bed about twelve midnight.

As Hurst finished, the Coroner, Dr Vaisey, expressed himself less than satisfied with his evidence, adding that he thought that Hurst was to a certain extent morally responsible for the crime, although to a lesser degree than King. Hurst and King, went on Dr Vaisey, had been constantly drinking together and this had no doubt been the cause of the crime. Hurst ought to be thoroughly ashamed of himself the Coroner declared and ought to take the occurrence as a warning to reform his conduct.

The landlady of the Swan public house, Mary Middleton, told the Inquest that she had served Albert King about 9.30pm on Thursday and he appeared quite sober then. After consuming two pints King had left, taking some draught beer in bottles with him.

A member of the Jury recounted seeing King come out of the Swan on Thursday night carrying the two bottles of beer but he had not walked off in the direction of Singleborough.

George Taylor, the carrier from Winslow, informed the Inquest that he had sold King a converted rifle for 12/6d the previous Tuesday, giving him four cartridges. King had told him that he needed it to shoot a fox with.

Sergeant Wootton stated that he had not only attended the scene of the crime but had also gone to Albert King's cottage at Singleborough and discovered that King's bed had not been slept in.

Dr Vaisey now addressed the Jury. He stressed that he did not believe one word of Hurst's testimony and it was his belief that Albert King had stayed the night at Hurst's cottage. He thought that Mrs King had been Albert's best friend and that on the fatal morning she had remonstrated with him and that he had shot her and then cut his own throat. If the Jury believed that Albert had killed Eliza King they must say it was murder and if they believed that he had been insane when he cut his own throat they could say so for it seemed that he had been verging on insanity for some time and that a man who drank as much as he did needed very little to make him so.

The Jury, with such a clear-cut recommendation, took only twenty minutes to return with the verdict that Eliza Jane King had been killed by her brother-in-law and that afterwards he had committed suicide.

A VERY PASSIONATE AFFAIR

Bourne End 1912

It must have seemed like sound common sense at the time for Mr and Mrs Hussey to take in a lodger. One of their daughters had moved out of their house on marrying George Jones of Furlong Road, Bourne End, and, with just one unmarried daughter, Dora aged seventeen years, it seemed like a good idea to supplement the family income by having a lodger. So it came about that one day in 1911 Phillip Trueman, then aged twenty-six years, a motor driver for a local firm, came to reside at the Hussey household. Had the Husseys been gifted with foresight and been able to foresee the tragedy that would eventually occur because of this one simple act, they would undoubtedly have left the spare room empty.

Over the next few months 'an acquaintance sprung up' between Trueman and Dora. There were 'seen out' together,

Furlong Road, Bourne End – where murder took place in 1912 – as it is today

49

often walking along the quiet county lanes around the village. After several months Trueman spoke to Mr and Mrs Hussey and asked to become engaged to their daughter. In an age when parental consent was all important Mr and Mrs Hussey at first withheld theirs but, after a while when still Trueman expressed his intention of marrying Dora, they relented. During the course of the following year, however, they had reason to reconsider their consent to the engagement.

Trueman changed in his attitude towards Dora, becoming extremely jealous and told her that he did not like her going out with any friends whether male or female. One in particular, Olive Carr, who had not only been at school with Dora but who also worked with her at the newsagents in Bourne End, would often go for long walks with her. Trueman told Olive that he did not approve of Dora going out with her and in future she was to go straight home from her work. One afternoon in early June of 1912, Olive had called for her friend and they had walked out together. At one stage they had turned and noticed that Trueman was following them. Making an excuse Dora had gone to him and they had both returned to her house.

Trueman bought little presents for his lover but even then showed a strange streak. Buying Dora a gold watch on one occasion he seized the one she already had and took it to pieces but never put it together again. One Sunday 23rd June, 1912 Miss Carr called for her friend, Trueman's decree notwithstanding, and the pair of them went out. When Trueman discovered this he went out straightaway and brought Dora back to the house in tears. As Mrs Hussey tried to console her daughter Trueman remarked, 'Dora has very much annoyed me.'

Mrs Hussey immediately retorted, 'In what way? She is young Mr Trueman and wants her freedom in her own way.' Trueman had no answer to that.

A few days later things took a decided turn for the worse. It was at breakfast time and Mrs Hussey, Dora and Trueman were present. It was time for Dora to leave for work but her fiancé would not let her go. There followed a conversation about the engagement which became rather heated. Eventually Trueman turned on his prospective mother-in-law and told her that she ought not to interfere with love affairs as it was not her place. Mrs Hussey immediately responded that Dora was far too young to become engaged and at this Trueman lost his temper and picking up a knife which lay on the table made some threatening gesture which caused poor Dora to burst into tears again.

Clearly matters could not go on in this way and Mr and Mrs Hussey discussed the issue with their daughter. It was decided that Dora should end the engagement. Consequently, on Saturday, 29th June, Dora handed back to Trueman all the presents he had given her before going to her job at Russell's the newsagent.

Nor was this all, for as Trueman left to go to his work Mr Hussey called him back and gave him a week's notice to quit his lodgings. The Husseys had also arranged for Dora to stay for the next few days with her married sister.

Rupert Russell, the owner of the shop where Dora and Olive Carr worked, knew that Dora was keeping company with Phillip Trueman, so he did not take particular notice when he called at his shop that Saturday morning and spent some minutes talking to her. After he had left however, Dora approached him, 'I was glad you were here Mr Russell.'

'Why, are you afraid of him? Would you rather than the boy stayed here?' enquired the somewhat bemused shop-keeper.

Dora's reply was immediate. 'I wish he would.'

Accordingly, Russell instructed his errand boy to stay in the corner and read a paper in case Dora's ex-fiancé returned. As the morning became afternoon and there was no sign of Trueman there was a more relaxed attitude in the shop. At about 5.30pm Dora called at her sister's house for tea. She told them that she had broken off the engagement between herself and Trueman. When they asked how he had taken it, she replied, 'Pretty well.'

Dora returned to the shop and during the course of the evening Trueman called in several times and spoke to her but nothing untoward happened, as Russell kept a watchful eye on them. He did see Trueman purchase some notepaper and envelopes. At 9 o'clock Dora eventually finished and Russell watched as she left his shop. He noticed that Trueman was waiting for her but when they both walked off in the direction of the Railway Station, assuming everything was now alright between the two he went indoors.

The next person to see the ex-lovers was Dora's brother-in-law, George Jones at 10.20pm as they both came to his house in Furlong Road. Dora left a small parcel at the house whilst Jones and Trueman had a chat by the garden gate. Trueman said, 'Me and Dora have had to part. It's hard to bear.'

Jones replied, 'Never mind old chap. It may be all for the best. It is the parents' wish.'

Trueman could only repeat, 'It is hard to bear.'

Dora emerged from the house and said, 'I'm just going up the road a few steps with him. I shall not be many minutes.'

Jones last words to his sister-in-law were, 'Don't be too long because it is late.' He then shook hands with Trueman and wished him, 'Goodnight', and watched them as they walked down the quiet road before turning into his house.

There were a number of people in Furlong Road that night including Mr and Mrs Weatherill. As they were walking along they heard a sound behind them and on looking round Weatherill saw what he took at first glance to be a drunken man. Weatherill went back to the man whom he recognised as Phillip Trueman. He saw that all was not well with him for he appeared to be smothered in blood from his jaw down to his waistcoat and he was making, in Weatherill's own words, '. . . a most peculiar noise.' Weatherill also noticed that he was waving either a razor or knife about in his hand. Weatherill abruptly turned about and went back to his wife and rushed her back to their home, warning others whom he encountered about a man who had cut his throat. As soon as he had put his wife in their home, Weatherill promptly informed the local Constable.

Other people had by now seen the strange apparition wandering about Furlong Road and went to assist him. One looking over a fence from which he thought the man had come saw a body lying there. On closer inspection it was discovered to be that of Dora Hussey.

A doctor was summoned to attend to Trueman and Dora but she was beyond all help, being quite dead.

Trueman was taken to the Cottage Hospital and a Police guard was put over him lest he should attempt to further injure himself. A letter was found on him, written on the notepaper bought at Russell's the newsagent earlier. It read, 'To Police and all concerned. I have been engaged to Dora my sweetheart for three months and I have spent £20 on her on different things and her mother and dad consented to our marriage and now they have gone and taken her away from me. I am under a week's notice from them. I cannot stand to be parted. I love the girl with all my heart and soul. I cannot bear it any longer. I am quite sane but I cannot live without my girl which is the purest in the world. God forgive my soul. God bless you and help you all in the world. I have nothing to live for. Your loving brother Phil.'

To one of the Constables watching at the hospital Trueman made a written statement. 'I did not mean to hurt Dora, I meant to commit suicide myself and she asked me to let her go with me. I kissed her before I did it. I did not let her suffer. Her father and mother both gave me their consent for me to have her about three months ago and then they broke it off. I kissed her just before I done it and she kissed me several times and said she wanted to go with me. I done it as soon as she said it. When I done it she dropped dead instantly.'

Trueman added, 'Oh dear, oh dear, why did I do it? Dora had her hands round my neck when I done it with a razor.'

Some days later when he was charged with murder and attempted suicide Trueman answered, 'I'm not guilty.'

He appeared at the Assizes on these charges in October and the question of Trueman's sanity was the prime factor in the trial. The jury could not decide on this and a new trial was ordered. In January 1913 Trueman was found guilty of the murder of Dora Hussey and sentenced to death. However, a few days later he was reprieved.

AMBUSH !

Botolph Claydon 1927

On the morning of Monday, 25th April 1927, men in villages all over the country were rising early and preparing themselves for a tedious day's labour. Two men in particular, however, would rise and leave their cottages that morning for the last time ever.

The Claydons are the villages which lie just a few miles from Buckingham. Steeple Claydon is the largest with East Claydon and Botolph Claydon next and finally Middle Claydon, which is hardly a village at all but which boasts that Claydon House, formerly the home of the Verney family and where once Florence Nightingale resided, lies within its bounds.

At Botolph Claydon, Edwin John Cook rose at 5am and took his wife a cup of tea as she lay in bed. A few minutes later, as he left, he called out, 'I shall be back at 9 o'clock,' adding that he then intended going to market. He cycled off in the direction of Knowle Hill Road to the small-holding which he rented from Sir Harry Verney.

Claydon House.

Botolph Claydon.

*Knowle Hill Road, Botolph Claydon – a murderer waited in
ambush for his victim.*

At nearby Middle Claydon, Joseph Beckett was also up and about. He told his wife that he was going to the spinney to shoot a rabbit and she reminded him that he must not be late for work. Beckett also made his way to Knowle Hill Road and secreted himself behind the hedge and waited patiently.

Edwin Cook slowly cycled along the quiet country road and if he had any thoughts they would probably have been on the jobs he knew he must do. He turned into Knowle Hill Road, which is in reality little more than a lane and made his way laboriously along it. Suddenly, from behind the hedge, came the roar of a shotgun and Edwin Cook, taking the full blast to the back of his head fell lifeless to the ground, still astride his bicycle. At sixty-three years of age, his life had been abruptly taken from him.

As the sound of the shot was carried away on the morning air, Joseph Beckett emerged from his hiding place and cautiously approached the still figure of Cook. Beckett looked down as the front wheel of Cook's cycle slowly revolved in its forks. Satisfied that he had completed the task he had set out to do, Beckett allowed himself a grim smile before turning and making his way back towards his cottage.

As he approached St. Catherine's cottages where he lived, he called out to his wife, 'Rose! Rose!' Mrs Beckett opened a window on hearing her name, no doubt wondering why her husband appeared so buoyed up.

Beckett looked up at her and shouted, 'Goodbye, I've killed someone!'

On hearing this amazing utterance, all Mrs Beckett could reply in her bemused state was, 'What have you done that for?'

Telling her to go back, Beckett waved his stick, then threw his gun into the air and, when he had caught that, threw his cap up in a state of complete exultation. As he walked off across the fields he turned and waved his hat as if in farewell to his wife.

Edwin Wise, a neighbour and nephew of Beckett, attracted by the commotion, gazed uncomprehendingly at his uncle's actions. He heard him shout at a passing cyclist, 'I have shot him!'

Wise called out, 'What's up?' but Beckett just answered, 'G'day old boy, I'm off.'

As he watched his uncle walk off across the field, he saw him remove first his jacket, then his waistcoat and throw them into the air. As he returned to his cottage, Wise next heard the sound of a shotgun and, turning, could only see his uncle lying in the field.

Abner Powell from nearby Catherine Farm was busy milking his cows when he was told that something dreadful had happened in the lane. Abandoning his work he went to where Cook's body lay, noticing that he still gripped the handlebars of his cycle. As he looked, Powell heard the sound of a shotgun being fired in the vicinity.

Police Sergeant Benning of Steeple Claydon was hastily informed and made his way to Knowle Hill Road. After arranging for Cook's body to be removed to his home at Botolph Claydon, Benning made a search at the scene of the murder and discovered a used cartridge behind the hedge. He also saw that the grass in the area had been trodden down by someone who had obviously spent some time there. As he looked up, Sergeant Benning also observed that anyone in that position would have been completely hidden from the view of persons using the lane.

Having been told of the finding of another body – the good Sergeant must have wondered how many more there were about the countryside that morning – Benning now went to where Joseph Beckett lay. He could see that he too was dead with a gunshot wound to the abdomen. Again, Sergeant Benning made a search and, looking in the pocket of the jacket which Beckett had discarded in his exuberance, found a piece of cardboard which bore the words, 'A life for a life. He likes to talk about other people's downfalls. God bless you and the three boys. They dared me to do this. Dear Rose, look after the boys as well as you can. God bless them. Goodbye.' On another part óf the cardboard was written, 'I have shot the man I hate.'

Benning also arranged for Beckett's body to be removed to his cottage and asked his widow if she recognised the writing on the cardboard. Mrs Beckett tearfully confirmed that it was in her husband's hand.

At the Inquest the next day, Mrs Cook was asked if Beckett had held any animosity towards her husband that would have in any way accounted for him taking his life. She answered that Beckett was jealous that her husband had the land to which he thought he was entitled, as his people had had it before. There had been words spoken between the two men some years ago about it, but Cook had said that it was Sir Harry Verney's right to let the land to whom he pleased.

After deliberating for a short time the Coroner's jury stated that Cook had been murdered by Beckett, who had then shot himself in a fit of temporary insanity.

'COULD I be SHOT INSTEAD of BEING HANGED?'

Beaconsfield 1949

PC143 Edward Ivory of the Buckinghamshire Constabulary yawned as he sat alone in Beaconsfield Police Station in the early hours of Saturday, 31st December, 1949. He had completed all the office tasks that habitually were done in the quietness of the middle of the night, and, as the telephone had not rung for some time, he poured himself a cup of tea and slowly drank it, fondly contemplating the warm bed he would be going to in a few short hours. The only sound to be heard was the steady tick-tock of the station clock.

A sudden hammering at the door, however, disturbed his reverie. Putting down his tea, he glanced up at the clock, saw that it was 3.45am and wondered what a caller could want at this unearthly hour.

Bower Wood – site of the Polish Re-settlement camp and where Maksimowski murdered Doreen Campbell.

The Constable opened the door and allowed his night-time visitor to enter. He saw that he was wearing a raincoat over a shirt and singlet and beneath his trousers he had on his pyjama trousers. As the man stepped into the light PC Ivory observed, with some curiosity, that he had his shoes on the wrong feet. The Policeman was even more puzzled when he saw that his caller's wrists had been cut and his hands were covered in blood! PC Ivory was more than a little astonished when the man stated in a thick East European accent, 'I have just killed a girl. She is in the forest.'

Recovering his composure, the Constable wanted to know more and, pointing to his wrists, the man went on, 'I did it with a razor,' adding sinisterly, 'I did the same with a girl in the woods. She is dead.'

PC Ivory now contacted Inspector Jennings, informing him of the strange caller. As quickly as he could the Inspector arrived. He too noted the state the man was in and in addition the fact that the man's clothing was bloodstained. More ominously he saw that his face was scratched.

By questioning him, Inspector Jennings ascertained that his

P. C. Ivory to whom Maksimowski surrendered himself.

name was Piotr Maksimowski and that he lived at the Resettlement Camp for demobilised members of the Polish Armed Forces at Great Bower Wood, about two miles from Beaconsfield on the Slough road. Inspector Jennings then asked Maksimowski what had happened, and in his slow hesitant English the Pole replied, 'A girl, she must be dead in the forest near the camp. We wanted to die. I cut her with a knife and razor. Then she didn't want to die. I cut myself. I put blanket over her. Now I come to Police Station.'

'What's the name of the girl?' the Inspector wanted to know.

'Doreen Campbell. She is married.' Maksimowski replied, adding that she lived in Shackelton Road, Slough.

Later, with a small team of Police Officers, Inspector Jennings took Maksimowski to Great Bower Rood where the Pole showed them the body of Mrs Campbell. She lay about two hundred yards from the main road, lying on her back, and, as Maksimowski had said, she was covered by a blanket. Her clothing was disarranged and an extensive pool of blood lay around her body. She had been stabbed and strangled and a doctor later explained that the clothing would have been disarranged by the deceased struggling for air and dying from loss of blood.

Maksimowski was taken back to the Police Station whilst PC Ivory was left to guard the woman's body. His thoughts as he stood alone with just a murdered woman for company in the middle of a dark wood, the wind blowing through the trees and unseen animals busy rustling in the undergrowth on a dark winter's night, can be imagined. It was not until daylight that he was relieved by another officer.

At Beaconsfield Police Station meanwhile, Maksimowski was being interviewed by Detective Sergeant William Ryan. In his halting English Maksimowski told the Policeman that he had known Mrs Campbell for about five months and had been seeing her two or three times a week. At first she had told him that she was a widow but he later found out that she was married. Maksimowski had met her husband at the Crown Hotel at Slough and there had been an argument, as a result of which Mrs Campbell had gone to the camp with Maksimowski and stayed there for three days before returning to her husband. Maksimowski had then arranged to meet Mrs Campbell at Windsor on December 30th. They had visited a number of public houses and both had consumed five whiskies and ten beers. They had left Windsor by train for Slough about 10.30pm. At Slough Railway Station Maksimowski had decided to take a taxi back to the camp alone. He had not wanted Mrs Campbell to go with him, he confided to Sergeant Ryan. However, she had jumped into the taxi first and would not take any notice of him when he tried to persuade her to go home. When they arrived at the camp, he went on, Mrs Campbell repeatedly asserted that he did not want her any more and was trying to get out of the situation whilst she still loved him. They had gone to the hut where he and three others slept. They had quarrelled and he had struck her, causing her to cry. He had then gone to bed but later got up and went to the wood with her, taking a blanket with him. Mrs Campbell then told Maksimowski that if they had to live together in this manner it would be better if they 'finished theirselves' now rather than later.

Maksimowski had agreed to this and as she could not kill him he would start with her. Mrs Campbell had then stretched out her hand towards her lover and shouted 'Finish!'.

Taking a knife from his pocket, Maksimowski continued, he had cut her wrist. She had not cried out but merely said that she was cold. Maksimowski had returned to the hut for a razor blade and another blanket. he came back to Mrs Campbell who by now was kneeling and crying, 'Why have you done it? It hurts.'

Maksimowski alleged that the blade had broken when he attempted to slash his own wrist. Mrs Campbell had then implored him to finish her off quickly because of the pain and Maksimowski had stabbed her in the throat with the knife and then in the back. During this, she was allegedly moaning, 'Pete, finish me, finish me.' He had then taken her by the throat and had started to choke her. Maksimowski repeated to the Detective that he had tried to cut his own wrist but the blade had broken. He had then decided to go to the Police.

When a doctor examined Maksimowski it was found that the cuts to his wrists were so slight that, once cleaned, they did not even require stitching.

A post mortem performed on Mrs Campbell revealed that she had been dead for some hours before her lover had raised the alarm at Beaconsfield Police Station.

Later the same morning Maksimowski was charged with murder and in reply said, 'I do not plead guilty to murder but I don't care about my own life. I admit I took the life from that woman.'

Maksimowski was swiftly committed and appeared at Warwickshire Assizes in March. The case was a foregone conclusion and he was found guilty after a short trial. After he had been sentenced to death, Maksimowski asked the trial judge if it were possible that the sentence might be varied from hanging to shooting. Mr Justice Croom-Johnson dismissed this by saying, 'I have no power to deal with it. It has passed out of my hands.'

Maksimowski was taken to the condemned cell at Winson Green Prison and the date of his execution was set for Wednesday, 29th March. A few days before, probably realising that all hope of a reprieve was lost, he attempted to commit suicide by running from one end of the cell to the other, jumping up at the cell window and by breaking the glass and thrusting his arms through had tried to slash his wrists on the jagged pieces of glass. The two Prison Officers guarding him had pulled him down and a doctor, after examining him, declared that he had not caused himself any serious injury. From then onwards an extra officer was placed in the cell.

Albert Pierrepoint was appointed as the hangman, with Syd Dernley assisting, and both men, on learning on Maksimowski's suicide bid, were apprehensive as they approached the condemned cell on the morning of 29th March, wondering how the prisoner would react. They had nothing to worry about for Maksimowski, now resigned to his fate, was marched from his cell to the execution shed and hanged, without causing any further trouble, in seven and a half seconds.

'I'D SOONER be RED than DEAD'
The Cosy Corner Stores Murder

Hazlemere 1950

For many years William Thomas Dearlove had kept a grocery and general provision shop called The Cosy Corner Stores at Sawpit Hill, Hazlemere, near High Wycombe. He had married in 1910, but he and his wife had separated some years later and from then on he had lived on his own. As so often happens to men who live without a woman's domestic touch, Dearlove had become somewhat reclusive and the rambling single storey corrugated iron and wooden stores and living quarters were later to be described as being in a filthy, dilapidated and ramshackle condition.

The only female who assisted him was nineteen year old Edna Norah Rackstraw, who called once a week to help him with his accounts. Despite being a lonely man Dearlove was generally well-liked by the people he served and he made an effort to be friendly with the inhabitants of the nearby Polish Re-settlement Camp.

On Saturday 8th July 1950, Dearlove worked all day in his stores as usual and late that evening was seen by a neighbour in a lane behind his shop. At 11am on July 9th, when Miss Rackstraw came to work on the accounts, she found the back door of the stores locked. Receiving no answer to her knocking, she left, only to return an hour and a half later. Again there was no response and, somewhat perplexed, she went home.

No one else could get a reply that Sunday, nor could they on Monday. It was not until 1pm that two delivery men from a local firm arrived with a consignment of confectionery and, seeing milk and papers lying uncollected on the doorstep, became curious. the van driver peered through a window at the rear of the premises and the mystery of why William Dearlove had not answered any of the callers became clear; for there on the floor behind the bed protruded a pair of legs. More ominously, on the bed could be seen a blood-stained pillow!

The Police were informed and the local Constable, PC Luker with Inspector William Foster promptly attended and broke into the bedroom. It was obvious to the Police Officers that Dearlove was dead and it was just as obvious that he had not died from natural causes, for his head bore unmistakable signs of wounds and his wrists and ankles had been tightly bound. As Inspector Foster looked round the bedroom he noticed that nearby lay a blue donkey jacket.

A murder investigation was initiated with Detective Inspector Kenneth Savin of the local CID commencing enquiries in the locality. After a conference later that day it was decided to ask for the help of Scotland Yard and Superintendent Mahon with Sergeant Foster duly arrived to co-ordinate the investigation. Also sent from the Yard was Superintendent Cherrill, head of the Fingerprint Bureau, who now made a detailed search of the stores and living quarters before returning to London with several photographs and articles for further examination.

Professor Keith Simpson arrived to perform the post mortem examination upon the body of Dearlove, whilst Dr W E Montgomery, principal scientific officer of the Metropolitan Police Laboratory, examined hairs and scrapings from the deceased's hands and fingernails. From the nail scrapings he removed certain dyed wool fibres.

Meanwhile Inspector Savin and his team were carrying out the necessary enquiries that have to be completed in any major investigation. The questioning of neighbours on the slight chance that they may have seen something of importance and the interviewing of people, who either called at the stores or who may have been in the area during the material times and who might have seen something suspicious, were carried out. In the course of these enquiries PC Luker spoke to a man who told him that he had seen two Poles, who had at one time lived at the Re-settlement Camp, hanging about the stores. Obtaining a description of them, Luker then saw the Camp Warden, who furnished the Police with the names of the two men he thought it could be, Zbigniew Kalinowski and Eugen Stefanowicz. The

Constable passed this information to Inspector Savin who in turn, realising its importance, communicated it to the two Scotland Yard Officers.

More Policemen were drafted in and the woods and fields in the vicinity of the Camp were scoured in an effort to trace these men, who it was thought at this stage might have been living rough in the area, but the search was unproductive.

The detectives also interviewed a friend of the two suspects named Stanislaw Piorkowski, a general labourer who lived at another Polish Re-settlement Camp at Great Bowerwood near Beaconsfield. Admitting that he had known Kalinowski and Stefanowicz for some time, he added that they were all chronically short of money and in fact Piorkowski and Stefanowicz had recently appeared at Court, pleading guilty to charges of burglary and housebreaking. During the afternoon of July 8th, he said both men had been at his hut. They mentioned that they had to appear before the Court for various debts and therefore they had to have some money. They said they were going to 'make a jump' in the High Wycombe/Hazlemere area. Whilst they were discussing this, another Pole, Wincenty Targosz, came into the hut. He pointed out to Piorkowski that there was a revolver in his locker. Piorkowski asked who had put the gun there and Stefanowicz replied, 'It is mine. I did it.'

, That evening, as the two almost destitute Poles left Piorkowski's hut, Stefanowicz took the revolver with him.

Next morning, about nine o'clock, the two men returned. Stefanowicz told Piorkowski that they had been somewhere about High Wycombe and Hazlemere and they had broken into a shop. Kalinowski butted in, 'Stefanowicz did wrong to that man.'

Stefanowicz said that they had done the job but added that he was not sure what had happened to the old man.

Kalinowski repeated, 'You have done wrong thing. You were very lucky to find the money.'

The two Poles made ready to leave Piorkowski's hut once more, but before they left Stefanowicz asked Kalinowski if he would go to Russia with him, adding, 'I have no choice. The old man may be alive or dead.'

Kalinowski responded, 'I am not going anywhere. I did not touch this man.'

The two men left. Piorkowski then gave Targosz a jacket and told him to take it into the woods. Most people, having been instructed to get rid of clothing, will, just before they do so, have a look through the pockets in case something of value has been left. Targosz was no exception. Possibly looking for money, all he found for his trouble was a piece of paper. An invoice addressed to someone called Dearlove!

On Monday, Piorkowski told the detectives he saw Stefanowicz and Kalinowski at the White Eagle Club in London. Stefanowicz was anxiously scanning the newspapers to see if the crime had been reported and what had happened to Dearlove. That was the last time Piorkowski had seen Stefanowicz.

This was good news for the detectives, and as a result Detective Inspector Rawlings and other Police officers called at 18 Diamond Road, Slough, where they saw Kalinowski. Informing him that he was being arrested on suspicion of murder, Kalinowski replied, 'I do not know anything about it because I was not there.'

Taken to High Wycombe Police Station, he was interrogated about the crime by Superintendent Mahon. Kalinowski at first denied that he was involved in the murder, stating that he had been at Piorkowski's hut during the night of July 8th–9th. However, realising that the Police had checked with Piorkowski, he eventually said, 'I did not kill the old man. I went to the shop with Stefanowicz. He killed him but I did not see him do it. I did not know the old man was dead until it was in the papers. Stefanowicz got into the shop and then opened the door and let me in. He had done something to the old man before he let me in.'

Kalinowski then made a long statement under caution wherein he admitted that he and Stefanowicz had discussed breaking into a shop as they were both short of money. Mention was made of the grocery shop and, when they left Bowerwood Camp, Kalinowski alleged that Stefanowicz had with him a revolver. They went by bus to Hazlemere and looked over the Cosy Corner stores for some time but he,

Kalinowski, got cold feet when Stefanowicz went around the back, leaving Kalinowski at the front of the premises. His initial reaction was to walk back to Bowerwood Camp but then he had realised it was too far and, seeing a lorry parked nearby, got into it and stayed there for the next two to three hours. He then went to the back of the shop where he had seen Stefanowicz go and saw him in the shed. Kalinowski alleged that Stefanowicz then said, 'I will go and see if I can open the door.' Kalinowski went on to say that he went to sleep and Stefanowicz woke him up, saying, 'We can go now.' Kalinowski asked if he had opened the door but Stefanowicz replied that he had found another way to get in and he would go inside and open the door for Kalinowski. This he apparently did, according to Kalinowski, who asked if there was anyone in the place, to which Stefanowicz told him not to worry as everything was alright. The pair of them had then searched the stores, staying until it was daylight. Stefanowicz, Kalinowski asserted, brought a small blue case into a room and the pair of them put the money they had found into it. Kalinowski informed the detectives that he noticed that there was blood on Stefanowicz's jacket. After they had filled the case Stefanowicz had gone into another room and, as he opened the door, Kalinowski had seen the body of a man lying on the floor.

'What is the matter?' he had said to Stefanowicz, who replied, 'I had something with this fellow,' which Kalinowski took to mean that he had had a struggle with the store-keeper. Kalinowski noticed that the hands of the man were tied and then Stefanowicz changed his clothing for some he found at the scene. Stefanowicz now put the revolver in the blue case along with the money. They left by way of the back door, which they locked, and began the long walk back to Bowerwood Camp, arriving there about 9am. Just before they reached the camp Stefanowicz took £10 out of the bag and handed Kalinowski half, adding that the rest of the money and the revolver was to remain in the case. Stefanowicz then went into the bushes and hid it. Stefanowicz had stayed at the camp and Kalinowski did not see him until Monday morning when he called at Kalinowski's lodgings in Slough. He gave Kalinowski £14.10s in silver, saying, 'That is yours.'

Kalinowski informed the Police that he next saw Stefanowicz at the White Eagle Club in London when Stefanowicz told him that there was £61 in the case. Kalinowski had next gone to the club on Wednesday but had not seen Stefanowicz and in fact he had not seen him since. He had bought some new clothes, and the £7 found on him by the Police at the time of his arrest was all that he had left.

So far so good, but the Police now wanted Stefanowicz very urgently. Warnings were sent to Police throughout the country and especially to those who had ports that had dealings with ships trading with the East European Communist bloc countries. Particular emphasis of course centred on the London docks, and enquiries revealed that Stefanowicz had fled the country having boarded a Russian ship, the Sestroretsk, which was bound for Leningrad via Kiel, Stockholm and other Baltic ports. Passengers who were travelling on the ship later recounted that Stefanowicz appeared an excellent companion for travelling with, speaking good English, German and Russian. When the ship arrived at Kiel, Inspector Donaldson of the Special Branch, on instructions from Scotland Yard, attempted to board the Destroretsk to remove Stefanowicz but was refused permission, whilst Stefanowicz looked on with amused interest from the deck. The Sestroretsk went on her way towards Stockholm, whilst a frustrated Inspector Donaldson communicated with Scotland Yard, who in turn made a request through the Foreign Office for Stefanowicz to be interviewed when the Sestroretsk reached the Swedish capital.

As the ship ploughed her way through the Baltic, one of the passengers was somewhat bemused when, in the middle of the night, he was awakened by the Sestroretsk suddenly lurching as it appeared to turn sharply.

Querying this with a sailor he was even more startled when he was informed, 'We are sailing in the wrong direction.'

He then decided to make his way to the bridge to ascertain what was happening, only to be apprised that they were rendezvousing with a Russian ship. About mid-day a Soviet tug came alongside and two Russian officers, one Army, one Naval, came aboard and went directly to the Captain's cabin.

For a while nothing much happened. Stefanowicz had lunch as usual, chatting cheerfully among the acquaintances he had met on the journey. Shortly after lunch, however, several passengers noticed Stefanowicz leaving the ship in the company of the Russian officers. The Sestroretsk then turned about and headed for Stockholm. It was only when they arrived there that they realised that the amiable Pole had in fact been wanted by the British police for murder!

The Foreign Office invited the Soviet Embassy in London to explain how a Pole who was wanted on suspicion of murder could leave this country in a Russian ship with the appropriate papers and be picked up at sea by a Russian tug when he could have been returned under normal extradition procedures. A spokesman gave the bland reply that Stefanowicz had presented himself at the Russian Embassy, stating that he had been born in Lithuania, then under Soviet domination, and wished to return. He was granted a repatriation certificate. It was pointed out that Stefanowicz had in fact been born in Poland and had registered in this country as a Polish labourer. The answer was a diplomatic shrug of the shoulders. As this was at the height of the Cold War there was really little more that could be done and Stefanowicz was home free.

It might be thought that that would have been the end of the matter as far as Stefanowicz was concerned, but a couple of months later a broadcast from Moscow Radio accused Britain of persecuting Stefanowicz. It was alleged that he had been recruited into British Intelligence and had been forced to join General Anders' White Army. He had then been sent to an Intelligence School for foreigners but, being unwilling to become a tool of the British Intelligence System, he had escaped, only to be systematically hounded by the British police. He had called at the Soviet Embassy in London and had requested to be repatriated to the USSR, which was how he came to be on board the Sestororesk when she sailed and to have been taken off by the Soviet tug. (No doubt he would now enjoy a perfectly free life in the Soviet Union, away from Police persecution.)

Having lost one suspect the Police concentrated on the one they had, and on Thursday, August 17th, Kalinowski appeared before High Wycombe County Magistrates Court for committal proceedings.

In his opening speech for the prosecution, Mr E C Jones read out the statement made by Kalinowski to the Police but added that, although it was substantially supported by the evidence, there were one or two discrepancies. Kalinowski alleged that he had gone to a lorry and then went to sleep in a shed but, said Mr Jones, in the premises, on a door leading from the shop, there was evidence that an effort had been made to effect an entry. The door-jamb had been broken and in the clothing that Kalinowski was wearing that night was found a piece of wood from that door in the turn-up of his trousers. That indicates, argued counsel, that Kalinowski was present when the door was being forced.

Mr Jones then went on with the further damning evidence that fibres from the blue pin-stripe suit that Kalinowski had been wearing the night of the attack had been found in the nail scrapings taken from the deceased. Also found in the bedroom was a blue donkey jacket which was heavily bloodstained and which, it was alleged, the accused had also been wearing.

Mr Jones went through the Prosecution's witnesses, including Professor Keith Simpson who told the Court of the results of his examination of the body. There were injuries to the face made with some considerable force probably with a fist; to the head made by an instrument and also injuries to the throat. When Professor Simpson had seen the body at the Cosy Corner Stores the hands and ankles were tied. This, in his opinion, had been done after death. Professor Simpson was shown a revolver taken from a small blue suitcase and again his opinion was that the wounds to the deceased could have been caused by such a weapon.

Mr William Docker of Slough then identified the bloodstained donkey jacket as his. The last time he had seen it had been in late June in his office on a building site at the Sewerage Works near Slough. Both Kalinowski and Stefanowicz had been employed there.

Wincenty Targosz gave his evidence of Piorkowski giving him a jacket on Sunday and instructing him to take it into the woods. This he had done, but he had rummaged through it first

71

and had come across an invoice belonging to Dearlove.

After hearing from a Detective Sergeant of examining the blue suitcase at Bowerwood Camp and discovering that it contained a revolver with ammunition, Kalinowski was committed for trial.

When he appeared at Aylesbury in October, it was pointed out to the jury that another person, who had escaped from this country, should have been sitting in the dock with him.

Again Professor Simpson went through his evidence of the injuries inflicted upon Dearlove and, shown a revolver, he repeated that some of the injuries could have been caused by it. Professor Simpson added that the throat injuries, which included a broken bone, had been caused by using considerable force whilst Dearlove was still alive, although whether he was conscious or not he could not say. His conclusion was that Dearlove had died from strangulation and suffocation from a gag which had been inserted into his mouth. In reply to defence counsel, Professor Simpson conceded that it was possible that Dearlove had been attacked, became unconscious and at some period had been attacked again. He was adamant that Dearlove had been alive when the gag had been placed in his mouth.

Janek Bandyra was the next witness and he said that three rounds of ammunition were found in a box of his which he had in a room he shared with Kalinowski in Slough. Under cross-examination he admitted having had the box for several years and had had it in huts he had shared with other men.

Dr W E Montgomery was shown a blue suit that Piorkowski had stated was similar to that worn by Kalinowski on the night of the murder. Seventeen wool fibres taken from the hands and nail scrapings of Dearlove were identical with the fibres of the blue suit. Dr Montgomery went further. There was also one pink cotton fibre similar to a pink stripe in the blue suit and a splinter of wood found in the trouser turn-up was similar to the wood of the back door of the shop. The trial judge, Mr Justice Stable asked if the fibres taken from the deceased's hands and nails could have come from any other article in the store which he had been asked to examine. Dr Montgomery replied emphatically that they could not.

Superintendent Guy Mahon, who next gave evidence, was forced to admit, when cross-examined, that anyone opening the door which had been broken at the store and squeezing through might pick up a splinter and agreed with defence counsel that it was easy to pick up things in a trouser turn-up. At the conclusion of the case for the prosecution, Mr C N Shawcross from the defence submitted that there was not sufficient evidence for a case to go before the jury on a charge of murder but conceded that there was evidence to support a charge of manslaughter.

Mr Justice Stable would not have that. 'It is murder or nothing,' he emphasised.

Kalinowski now made the short journey from the dock to the witness box. Led by his counsel speaking mainly in English but occasionally assisted by an interpreter Kalinowski told the Court that he had been a boy when the Germans had invaded his country and he had been wounded in the battle for Warsaw. Later on he had been put in a forced labour camp where he had endured terror and brutalities. He did not know what had become of his parents. In 1945 he had escaped from this hell and joined the Polish Army in Italy and had eventually arrived in England where he had stayed ever since.

Having hopefully engaged the sympathy of the jury, Kalinowski was led carefully through his evidence by his counsel. He had first met Stefanowicz in October 1947 when he had lived at the Resettlement Camp at Bowerwood near Beaconsfield. He had left the camp to go into lodgings in Slough owing £30 in maintenance but by July he had managed to reduce that sum to £17.

He then went on to relate the events of the fatal night which were in accord with the statement given to the Police. There was a dramatic moment when, on the instructions of his counsel, Kalinowski donned the trousers of the blue suit he had been wearing when arrested and the donkey jacket, stained with blood, which had been found at the scene of the murder. He stood on a chair so that the jury could clearly see him. Mr Shawcross said, 'It is suggested that you were wearing the coat while assaulting the man and while doing so got blood on it?'

Kalinowski replied, 'No.'

'Was there ever a spot of blood on your trousers?' asked Mr Shawcross.

'I never saw any spot,' replied Kalinowski.

Kalinowski stated that when received into prison he was examined and no bruises or other marks were found on any part of his body.

Mr Shawcross asked his client to recount the events of that fateful night, 'Before we go to this place, Stefanowicz tell me where he will go in the night time when this man will be asleep and he tell me where he will go inside and take the money and that will be very easy. I did not think there would be struggle.'

Answering questions put to him by Mr Justice Stable, Kalinowski swore that he had not seen the body of Dearlove on the floor until after Stefanowicz came back with the money. He had seen the revolver in Stefanowicz's hand before he returned with the money, it was then broad daylight. He had not gone into the room where the body was, but saw it through the doorway two or three yards from it. The man's face was covered. He saw no movement and heard no sound from the body.

Mr Justice Stable asked him, 'Did you take any step whatever to find out what condition that body was in?'

'No,' was the reply.

'Was it perfectly apparent to you that that man was either dead or grievously injured?'

'When I saw him I thought this man was alive. I thought his hands were tied up and his mouth was covered up to avoid any shouts.'

The closing speeches now began. Mr Fearnley-Whittingstall for the prosecution said that if Kalinowski knew that Stefanowicz was armed or knew he was prepared to use violence, then if Stefanowicz committed murder without Kalinowski being inside the stores when the struggle took place, Kalinowski would be guilty of murder. Counsel also submitted that Kalinowski must have lent some part to the assault, for it was impossible for fibres from his suit to have got into the dead man's fingernails and onto his hands if he had taken no part in his murder.

Mr Shawcross then faced the jury. There was no reliable and untainted evidence that Kalinowski knew Stefanowicz had a revolver or that he might use violence, he said. Mr Shawcross alleged that the prosecution's case was entirely misconceived and depended largely, though not entirely, on circumstantial evidence. Mentioning the donkey jacket he said that it was quite possible that Stefanowicz had worn it at the time of the assault and had taken it off before returning to the stores again, which would account for the fact that he had bloodstains on his suit. It was unthinkable that Kalinowski had been wearing it and not have got blood on his trousers. As for the tiny splinter of wood found in his trousers, that could have got there in a hundred and one different ways.

Mr Justice Stable, in summing up, pointed out the law of common design by one or more persons to use violence in the commission of a felony, and if as a result human life was taken each person was equally responsible in the eyes of the law and each was guilty of murder. If, however, they believed Kalinowski's evidence they would acquit him.

The jury retired but after only twenty-five minutes returned with a verdict of Not Guilty.

Kalinowski stepped from the dock a free man. He collected his belongings from the Prison Officers, walked from the cells underneath the Assize Court – and was promptly re-arrested by Police who conveyed him to High Wycombe where he was charged with breaking into the house of Dearlove and stealing a case containing clothing and money. When he appeared before the Magistrates' Court his response in answer to the charge was, 'Can I have the solicitor I had before?'

Kalinowski was once more committed to the Bucks Assizes where he appeared in January 1951. He pleaded guilty to this charge and was sentenced to twenty-one months imprisonment.

TWO RED CARNATIONS for a BLUE LADY

Slough 1954

In 1896 Trooper Charles Wooldridge, in a fit of passion, had cut the throat of his wife (whom he had originally met whilst stationed at Windsor with the Royal Horse Guards) because he suspected her of infidelity. He then surrendered himself to the Police and was tried, convicted and sentenced to death. Whilst awaiting execution he was immortalized by Oscar Wilde, who was serving a sentence of imprisonment at the same time, in his 'Ballad of Reading Gaol'. Almost sixty years later another trooper with the same regiment was to commit murder under almost identical circumstances.

Thomas Walton aged twenty years of C Squadron, Royal Horse Guards was courting a girl of eighteen. She was Audree Wilson and she lived with her family at 13, Devon Avenue, Slough. A lodger, Martin O'Sullivan, completed the household. The Wilson family had moved to the area from Thornaby on Tees some three years before and, after attending a local school,

Devon Avenue, Slough – as it is today.

Audree was working as an invoice clerk with a firm on the nearby Trading Estate. She had been engaged to another trooper when she met Walton but broke it off in favour of her new admirer.

Matters seemed to be progressing well between the two young lovers, for in September 1954 they became engaged and Walton mentioned to one of Audree's brothers that he intended buying a caravan so that they could live together. They hoped to be married at Christmas. However, the path of true love never did run smooth and cracks began to appear in the romance. It may be that Audree realised that she was too young to embark on a lifetime's commitment to one man. Whatever the reason, quarrels had occurred between the two and although Audree might not be as enthusiastic as before, her fiancé was, for he still pursued her with undiminished ardour.

On Saturday, October 9th, Walton had telephoned Audree to tell her that he was unable to meet her. Later he had 'phoned again to say that he could meet her, but Audree had replied that it was no use him going over to Slough as she was going shopping with a girl-friend. Walton had been annoyed by this and had remarked to a colleague that if Audree had stood him up for one of her friends he was not going to go over to see her and she could ring him up whenever she thought differently.

In a local café two nights later Walton met a fellow trooper, Ivor Emmens, who expressed surprise that Walton was not seeing Audree. 'No,' Walton told him, 'we have had an argument.' He added that he was waiting for her to ring him as he did not want to lower his pride by telephoning her and asking her to go out with him again. A few minutes later he was alleged to have murmured, 'If I can't have her, no-one else will.'

The next afternoon Walton approached Emmens in the cook-house at the barracks and enquired if there was a grindstone in the butcher's shop. On being told that there was, Walton left, returning a few minutes later to show Emmens a knife and asked him if it was sharp enough. Emmens glanced at the knife and nodded. As he turned to leave, Emmens thought he heard Walton mumble, 'This will make a mess of her.'

At 6pm the same evening, October 12th, O'Sullivan, the lodger, bumped into Audree in the bathroom they shared at the Devon Avenue house and had a short conversation with her before she went to her bedroom. Shortly after, O'Sullivan saw Walton in battledress on the landing, holding two fresh carnations. O'Sullivan was somewhat surprised at this, because a few days earlier the trooper had told him that he did not think he would be calling anymore, as he and Audree had been fighting. When Walton asked if Audree was around, O'Sullivan replied somewhat non-commitally that he did not know. Walton was not deterred by this evasive answer and entered Audree's bedroom. O'Sullivan went down to the living room.

Fifteen minutes later he heard footsteps running down the stairs and the sound of the front door being slammed shut. He next heard Audree's younger brother Jimmy call out and O'Sullivan rushed upstairs to Audree's bedroom. He saw Audree laying on her bed, her face covered in blood. Although first aid was attempted and a faint pulse could be felt, by the time an ambulance had arrived and she was conveyed to Upton Hospital, Audree Wilson had died.

At 6.32pm WPC Tompkins, on duty at the telephone switchboard at Slough Police Station, received a call from a breathless man, 'Please send a police car to the Ambassador, Farnham Road'. Obtaining his name, WPC Tompkins asked why he wanted a police car sent to the cinema. 'I have just killed a girl!' was the startling reply.

As quickly as she could, the WPC notified the Information Room of the Bucks Constabulary at Aylesbury, who in turn passed a message out to one of the Motor Patrol cars cruising Slough Division.

The driver, PC Douglas Windsor and his 'observer' PC James 'Jock' Gallacher immediately made their way through the traffic in their sleek black Riley patrol car. As they came to a halt at the cinema forecourt, Walton approached the car and asked, 'Are you looking for me?'

In his thick Scottish accent, PC Gallacher replied, 'Yes. Get in the back of the car.'

Walton climbed in and sat down as directed. 'I am the bloke you are looking for,' he confirmed. 'I have just killed my girl with this.' He produced a blood-stained 'dagger' which PC Gallacher carefully took from him. PC Windsor put the car in gear and sped off in the direction of Slough Police Station. With a certain sense of irony Walton remarked to the two Police Officers, 'A lot of things have happened since Six.'

On his arrival at the Police Station Walton was informed that Audree was at the hospital. 'I hope she is dead', was his only comment. As PC Gallacher waited with his prisoner for the CID to take over, Walton reflected, 'She two-timed me and when she laughed at me, I let her have it.'

Gallacher asked Walton where he had obtained the knife. 'I have had it for years,' he answered.

Detective Inspector Robert Almond now took charge of the investigation and went straightaway to 13, Devon Avenue. As he entered Audree's bedroom he noted that the bedclothes and pillows were saturated with Audree's blood, that there were splashes of blood on the wall and a pool of blood lay on the floor. All this suggested to the detective that a frenzied attack had taken place. On the bed he also discovered a white ear-ring, a brooch and the broken pieces of a black belt. On the floor he found the matching ear-ring, the knife sheath and two fresh carnations in the shape of a button-hole.

Inspector Almond returned to Slough Police Station where he interviewed Walton and took a statement from him. 'It all started in May last year,' the trooper informed the Inspector. 'I was introduced to Audree by some friends. She was engaged and her fiancé was away. I liked her and asked her to see me. She agreed and I saw her pretty often. Almost every day. She'd agreed to break off the engagement but waited until he came back in July last year and she did break it off. I have seen her nearly every night since. We used to have little quarrels but they were soon patched up. About six weeks ago she began to get restless and the rows became more frequent. Last Saturday we had a row on the telephone. I thought she'd been out with someone else on the Friday. I was mad and I did not see her for a couple of days. Today I thought I would come over and patch it up. I brought some flowers as I usually do after a row. I went round to her home . . . I let myself in. Audree was upstairs. She was in her bedroom and I went in and gave her the flowers.

I could see she was all dressed up and ready to go out. I asked where she was going. She said the fun was over and she was going back to her fiancé. I asked why she had suddenly decided to make the change. She laughed and said, "It wasn't sudden." She said she was tired of stringing me along and that whenever I was on duty or away she was a one-night stand for any man who liked to pick her up. When she said that, I just saw red. The next thing I remember she was lying on the bed with blood all over her and me, the sheets and the wall. I went downstairs, went straight out the front door and along the road. I looked down at my hands and saw they were covered with blood and the knife was still in my hand. I went to the kiosk and phoned the Police and told them I had just killed a girl and asked them to come and fetch me. They told me to wait. When they came, I told them I was the person who had called. I got in the Police car and they brought me down to the Police Station. The knife is mine. I used to do a bit of carving with it but I haven't had much time for it and had almost forgotten about it. This morning I found it in my locker and as there was a big inspection coming off I didn't want it lying around. It was in a bad condition so I cleaned it and put it in my pocket. I meant to dump it here.'

Walton was charged with murder and appeared at Slough Magistrates' Court where he was committed to Birmingham Assizes.

At his trial Walton denied having the conversation with Emmens in the cookhouse or making the remarks which now seemed so incriminating. He had only tried to sharpen the knife, he said, because it was rusty. He had gone to Audree's after buying some flowers, he added, and went on to describe what had taken place at 13, Devon Avenue that fateful night as he had to Detective Inspector Almond in his statement.

Asked by his counsel, Mr Claud Duveen, what he had meant when he had said at the Police Station that he hoped that Audree was dead, Walton answered, 'I didn't like to think of her in blood lingering on.'

'Had you any intention of killing Audree Wilson?' asked Mr Duveen.

'No, sir!' the trooper replied emphatically.

*Audree Wilson and
Trooper Thomas Walton
in happier times.*

'At any time?'

'No, sir!'

After Walton had been subjected to cross-examination several witnesses appeared to testify as to the state of the trooper's mind. The jury listened patiently to their evidence and then the addresses by the defence and prosecution barristers and the Judge's summing up. After a short adjournment they returned with a verdict of Guilty.

Walton was sentenced to death and an appeal was made but turned down. A petition was got up and submitted to the Home Secretary. With only a few days left before he was due to meet the hangman the Home Secretary announced that the sentence would be commuted.

It must surely have been a coincidence that, on the week following the arrest of Trooper Walton outside the Ambassador cinema, the management were showing a film called 'The Lovers'.

The ODIOUS Mr REGAN

The Britwell Murderer 1962

When Anthony O'Rourke arrived in Pickering with his wife, Florrie, and children in 1949, he appeared, to the inhabitants of this pleasant bustling town which lies at the foot of the North Yorkshire moors, a quiet, meek-looking Irishman who could do no ill to anyone. Everything was not as it seemed however for what they did not know was that Florrie was not actually his wife, as he had bigamously married her some years before and for that offence he had served a period of imprisonment. He also had convictions for cashing forged cheques and for child neglect. He had moved to the area in the hope of leaving this behind him and the usually canny Yorkshire people suspected nothing of the newcomer's past. At first the O'Rourkes lived at 10, Willowgate, the home of an elderly man named Tom Pickering, but then left for lodgings at 129, Westgate, where a middle-aged spinster, Rose Hannah Harper, resided. After a short stay there O'Rourke moved his family to a damp, derelict basement cut into the cliff in the shadow of Pickering Castle. It was a hovel and totally unfit to settle in, especially with children, as it had no water or sanitation and was hardly an improvement on the two previous addresses they had stayed at.

Shortly after mid-day on Saturday, 5th November, a Mrs Fenwick of 9, Willowgate noticed O'Rourke walking down the road. As she watched

Anthony Regan.

him from her doorstep she saw him hesitate then turn around. She called out, 'Don't you know it's unlucky to turn back?' O'Rourke smiled at her but said nothing and, after he had taken a quick look around the quiet street, Mrs Fenwick saw him cross over and enter his old lodgings.

Just under an hour later another resident of Willowgate saw O'Rourke walking along the street coming from the direction of number 10.

At 4.30pm the old age pensioner who now lodged with Tom Pickering returned and tried to enter the house, but found the door locked. This was somewhat unusual, as was the fact that the curtains of the house were drawn to. Assuming that Pickering had gone out, he decided to wait outside for his return.

Some five hours later, this patient lodger was still waiting, but he had been noticed by Mr Fenwick and others who came and tried the door for themselves. They too found it locked but as their hearing was much sharper than the old lodger's they could hear groaning coming from inside the house. Fenwick broke a window and climbed in. Fetching a light he saw Pickering lying on the floor, his skull smashed in and his face covered in blood. The only door had been locked, apparently from the outside, and, as no key could be found, Fenwick had to break it open to allow the others in. On the floor near the door was a bloodstained poker; there was a pool of blood by the fireplace and all around the room there were bloodstains.

Old Tom Pickering was taken to hospital and when he was examined by a doctor he was found to have a trough-shaped depression on the crown of his head which appeared to have been caused by a heavy blow with a blunt instrument, probably the poker. Splinters of bone from the skull had entered his brain and an emergency operation was performed for their removal.

When the Police were informed of the circumstances and had carried out their initial enquiries they were, of course, very anxious to interview O'Rourke and went to his address in Castlegate where they saw his 'wife' Florrie. Their quarry was not there and Florrie either could not or would not tell them where he had gone.

Whilst the Police were commencing their search for O'Rourke he had called at a snack bar at Scarborough and had used one of Pickering's old age pensioner's tobacco coupons.

When this came to light, extensive enquiries were carried out in the seaside resort but without success and nothing more was heard of O'Rourke for several days until a letter-card was delivered for Florrie, postmarked 'Stockton-on-Tees'.

The Police seized and carefully studied it.

'My darling wife and babies,

Just a line hoping you and the children are keeping well and happy as it leaves me same at time of writing. Well, I am sorry for what happened but I got sick of people saying things about you and he said that he had been with you and that got me. As you know I love you. I will not let anyone say it to my face. I did it for you, Florrie. Please see me where – works at the cabin on Friday night at eight-thirty. I love you and more. Don't let anyone see this letter. Love Tony.'

Enquiries now moved to the Stockton area but O'Rourke managed to elude his pursuers and travelled back to Pickering on a bus, returning to his family where he stayed for a few hours before the Police arrived and detained him. His reply on being arrested was, 'I didn't think I'd hit him so hard.'

On his arrival at the Police Station he was charged with wounding with intent to cause grievous bodily harm. He made a brief statement in which he admitted going to Pickering's house where an argument had broken out between the two men and Pickering had started calling him names and he, O'Rourke, had then struck the old man about the head and face.

Tom Pickering, meanwhile, was still clinging to life and at first after his operation he had seemed to be on the way to recovery. However, as sometimes happens his condition took a turn for the worse and it was decided to take a dying declaration from him. Accordingly, in the presence of O'Rourke and a magistrate, a deposition was obtained in which he stated that he had been sitting down in his house when O'Rourke had arrived. They had been talking for a while when something had gone wrong; something went bang on his head. He had been unable to get up and he had asked O'Rourke to open the door which he would not do. He saw that blood was pouring down his face but he was unable to work out how he had come by the bump on his head. He had not seen O'Rourke carrying anything and he did not think he had had an argument with him.

Tom Pickering survived for over a month after the attack but finally succumbed to his injuries on 15th December. O'Rourke was now charged with his murder.

To John Parris, one of the barristers briefed to defend O'Rourke, it appeared a hopeless task. As he admitted in his memoirs, '. . . the apparent cold-blooded callousness of O'Rourke was calculated to revolt a jury. It appeared to be an assault on an old man by a young one and a brutal assault at that with a poker . . . and O'Rourke, even when he saw Pickering covered in blood, had ignored his pleas, had drawn the curtains, locked the door and walked off with the only key, leaving the old man to stagger about in his own blood for at least eight hours. And what would the jury make of O'Rourke having taken the old man's tobacco coupon and having cashed it the very same day? And of that letter to Florrie ". . . hoping you and the children are keeping well and happy as it leaves me same at the time of writing".'

What made the situation seem even worse was that when O'Rourke was seen by his solicitor and his proof of evidence taken, he denied that he had been anywhere near the house that day or that it was he who had struck Pickering. This, despite having been seen going and coming from his house. Also the fact that he had run away from his own house would not aid him at all.

Parris saw him in prison and pointed out to him that he was in dire straits if he persisted with the nonsense he had fed his solicitor. O'Rourke agreed and when he was seen the next week by Parris he had written out an entirely new statement.

On his appearance at Leeds Assizes early the following year the prosecution presented their case of a savage and brutal murder effected by a blow with a poker on the scalp of the defenceless old man. Much emphasis was placed on O'Rourke's conduct after the fatal blow had been struck and even his Counsel began to think that a guilty verdict must be returned.

Then Florrie was called to give evidence for the prosecution. She told of O'Rourke's absence from home from the 5th November until the 13th. Of how she had lived with O'Rourke for years, some of that time in Pickering's house, and she identified the letter written to her by O'Rourke whilst he had been on the run.

The defence now cross-examined her. She stated that whilst living with Pickering he had tried to seduce her, she had resisted and he had turned nasty. She had not told O'Rourke of this but now the sentence in the letter, '. . . He said that he had been with you and that got me', became suddenly clear and the deceased, in the eyes of the public attending the trial and more importantly the jury, turned from a helpless old age pensioner into a 'dirty old man' who had made indecent advances towards his young female lodger.

At last O'Rourke went into the witness box. He had, he informed the Court, not the slightest reason to quarrel with Pickering, in fact they had always been on friendly terms. However, on the 5th November as he was walking home Pickering had called him into his house and told him that he had received a letter from O'Rourke's mother concerning Florrie. Pickering had then, alleged O'Rourke, began to abuse Florrie saying she was no good; that he had been with her and that he had given her money for her sexual favours. O'Rourke had become incensed and they had argued. Pickering had then grabbed his pullover and they both had fallen across the fender in front of the fire with Pickering on top of him. The old man had grabbed the poker which was lying nearby and was about to strike O'Rourke when he took it from him and got his blow in first. Pickering had groaned and rolled over into the fireplace. O'Rourke had fled the scene but as he rushed out of the house he had noticed a piece of paper on the floor and thinking he dropped it he had picked it up. Later he discovered that it was Pickering's tobacco coupon.

Despite all this there were many questions left unanswered. If, as he was now putting forward, this had all happened whilst he was defending himself why had he made no mention of it before, least of all to Florrie? Why had he drawn Pickering's curtains? Why had he locked the door of the house and taken the key? Why had he run away and not informed the Police of what he now alleged took place? Why had he cashed Pickering's tobacco coupon? What had he lived on whilst on the run? The old man's savings? How had a fit young man found himself almost overcome by a feeble old man?

O'Rourke's cross-examination never elicited the complete answers to all these questions but apparently served only to establish his credibility. After the closing speeches by counsel and the Judge's summing up the jury retired, returning after two-and-a-half hours with a Not Guilty verdict. O'Rourke had left the dock before his astonished counsel could turn round in his seat.

It would be some time later that Florrie admitted to Parris that the story she had told in the witness box about Pickering seducing her had been concocted between O'Rourke and herself the night he had returned before being apprehended by the Police. 'I didn't want to do it,' she told Parris, 'but I couldn't let my husband hang, could I?' With hindsight, it might have been better if she had told the truth.

Months passed; they were not easy for the O'Rourkes as can be imagined living in such a close-knit community. They were ostracized by the towns-people, who would cross the street rather than meet them and were by and large ignored and left to fend for themselves.

On June 4th 1951, Rose Harper, the fifty-five year old spinster living at 129 Westgate and with whom the O'Rourkes had lodged for a while before they moved into Castlegate, called at her neighbour's to borrow her teapot before she threw away the tea leaves. She would refill it with hot water in order that she herself might have a cup or two or tea. She returned the teapot half an hour later.

Nothing more of her was seen that day and by 9pm some friends of hers, Mr and Mrs Pashby, being somewhat concerned went round to her cottage. The front door was locked but Mr Pashby fetched a ladder and entry was gained through a bedroom window. The upstairs was in a state of great disarray as though someone had been searching the rooms. Mr Pashby made his way downstairs, wondering what he might encounter. The living room was also in an untidy state although not as bad as the room she had just visited. Of Miss Harper, there was no sign.

The Pashbys now went to the Police Station and returned to the cottage in Westgate with a Police Sergeant. Darkness had fallen by now and as there was no gas or electricity laid on at the cottage the Sergeant had to look around by candlelight. He could find no trace of Miss Harper either and it was assumed by all parties that she had gone out and had not yet returned.

About midnight a somewhat inebriated Tony O'Rourke approached a Scarborough taxi-driver and requested to be driven to Pickering and on arrival at that town directed the driver to 129 Westgate. O'Rourke explained that it was his mother's house and that he wanted to remove some items to his sister's place. The taxi-driver watched as O'Rourke went to the front door, unlocked it and entered the cottage, emerging a few minutes later with first a wireless set, then a sewing machine and finally with some bedding, all of which was loaded onto the taxi. The driver was then instructed to drive to Castlegate where all the articles were removed. When he asked for his fare O'Rourke said that he had no money but handed him a watch and chain, adding that he would settle up with him next week. Realising that he would get no money that night from his strange customer he drove back to Scarborough.

At 6.30am the next day O'Rourke presented himself at the town Police Station where he spoke to the Police Sergeant who had visited 129 Westgate the previous evening, 'I killed Rose Harper yesterday,' he told the astonished Sergeant, who then took him before his Inspector who expressed his incredulity quite forcibly whilst the Sergeant voiced his doubts by stating that he had searched the cottage and could not find Miss Harper.

'You'd better go and have another look,' O'Rourke advised the two Policemen.

Off went the Sergeant and, in the cold light of day, he could see a pair of bare feet sticking out from under a table. Moving a chair the Sergeant pulled away a rug covering the body of Rose Hannah Harper. Returning to the Police Station the Sergeant informed the Inspector of his discovery.

'There, what did I tell you,' said the smug O'Rourke.

A full scale murder investigation now commenced and one of the first officials at the scene was a pathologist who believed that Miss Harper had been dragged to the spot where she had been found. A handkerchief had been rammed into her mouth and a stocking had been tied tightly around her neck. He also noticed that considerable force had been used against her as there were marks to her throat and both thyroid bones had been broken. It was his opinion that her attacker had used one hand to grip her throat whilst the other hand held the back of her neck.

All that O'Rourke would tell the Police was, 'I killed her with my hands and pushed her under the table at her home.' This was dutifully taken down in writing and O'Rourke signed it.

The Police were diligent in their enquiries and found witnesses who had seen O'Rourke strolling in the direction of Rose Harper's cottage about the time that she had collected the teapot from her neighbour and then, about three-quarters of an hour afterwards, had seen him walking in the opposite direction whilst later he had been observed boarding a Scarborough-bound bus.

Naturally O'Rourke wanted the same lawyers who had represented him at the previous trial and somewhat reluctantly John Parris visited him once again in Armley Gaol. O'Rourke handed his barrister six pages of notes and whilst Parris expressed his doubts about the case, O'Rourke was optimistic about its outcome.

For the second time in two years O'Rourke appeared in the same courtroom at Leeds Assizes charged with a capital offence.

The motive for the murder of this woman who had been a good friend to O'Rourke was robbery, suggested prosecuting counsel, for he had stolen her wireless, her sewing machine and her bedding. Even the watch and chain he had given to the taxi-driver in payment of the fare had been stolen from Miss Harper's cottage.

The prosecution went through their case witness by witness until it was the turn of the defence. Parris called O'Rourke into the witness box and all eyes in the Court now fastened upon him.

He agreed that he had been on friendly terms with Rose Harper since the family had lived with her before moving to Castlegate. He had, he said, bought various items from her: a wireless set, a sewing machine and bedding but she had not handed them over. One Sunday night in June she had called on the O'Rourkes to borrow some sugar. The subject of the purchased items had cropped up and she had told O'Rourke to call at her cottage early the next day to collect them. Accordingly he had walked round to see her on Monday morning and Miss Harper had mentioned that the sewing machine was in the bedroom. He followed her upstairs to retrieve it when she had suddenly attacked him, forced him onto her bed and had suggested that he have sexual intercourse with her. He had struggled and tried to reason with her and finally managed to break free of her amorous clutches and had made his way downstairs where she had followed him. She now offered to make him a cup of tea which he accepted but then she had started to abuse Florrie, calling her foul names and insinuating that she had had intercourse with other men, receiving payment for so doing. O'Rourke went on by saying that he had responded and Rose Harper had become really angry and had attacked him again, this time grabbing hold of his genitals and causing him some considerable pain. He had tried to push her away but she had a firm grasp and would not release him. In a final desperate act he had then placed his hand around her throat. Strange to relate, not only did Rose Harper release her hold on his private parts, but also her whole body went limp and slumped to the floor. He had then panicked when he saw her lying still, for he maintained that he had not intended to harm her. He had then placed a handkerchief in her mouth and tied it securely in position with a stocking in case she regained consciousness and started screaming. He had left and walked around Pickering in a quandry before deciding to go back to the cottage to see if she had recovered. She had not and as he took the stocking from around her face he realised for the first time that she was not breathing. She was, in fact, quite dead!

He determined to leave once more but went upstairs to see if he could find the £16 he had given her for the articles. He could not and locking the front door behind him had made his way to a bus stop and thence to Scarborough where he had spent all day drinking. He had, he agreed, returned by taxi to Pickering at the end of the day and taken the items to which he felt he was entitled and had paid the taxi-driver with a watch and chain.

Naturally the prosecution challenged him strongly in cross-examination, especially with regard to the positioning of the stocking on Miss Harper, but O'Rourke was adamant that he had placed it around her mouth and had only moved it to around her neck after he discovered that she was already dead. He could not say if he had tied it around her neck tightly or not. When asked why he had gone to the Police the following morning, O'Rourke explained, 'I did not want anyone else to get blamed. That was why I gave myself up'.

It was by all accounts a strenuous cross-examination but O'Rourke bore up well under the relentless questioning and managed to convey an air of truthfulness about his answers.

At the close the prosecuting counsel in their summing up attempted to portray O'Rourke as an inveterate liar who had wilfully killed a woman who had befriended him.

O'Rourke's counsel, in mitigation, argued that as he was friendly with the deceased, he had no reason to kill her. There was no evidence of malice or a desire for revenge. He had not gone to her house 'like a thief in the night' and broken in and the medical evidence had shown that Rose Harper had died in less than a minute and not by a slow deliberate strangling. Furthermore it was shown that O'Rourke had, on admission to Prison, been seen to be suffering from a rupture which might have been caused by an attack on his genitalia as he had alleged.

The jury were, after the Judge's summing up, absent for about half an hour before returning. Parris admitted to a feeling of foreboding as he stole a quick glance at his, by now, ashen-faced client in the dock. Looking back up to the Bench he saw the Judge's clerk stand poised with the black cap ready to place it in position.

The Clerk of the Assize rose and addressing the foreman of the jury asked if they had found the prisoner guilty or not guilty of the murder of Rose Hannah Harper.

'Not Guilty', came the astonishing reply.

Parris heard a gasp come from O'Rourke behind him, before the foreman announced that the jury had found him guilty of her manslaughter.

Mr Justice Pearson did not mince his words when he addressed the prisoner after he had heard the Police give evidence of his previous convictions and knowing full well that he had appeared at the same Court only a short time before on a murder charge and had been acquitted. 'It is a bad manslaughter showing considerable callousness and brutality. You have some criminal record. The sentence of this Court is that you be imprisoned for ten years.'

'Oh no!' gasped Florrie and had to be assisted from the Court by a Policewoman.

'Better than winning the first prize on the pools', remarked O'Rourke to the Prison Officers as he was led down to the cells.

Parris went down to see him and asked him what had really happened.

'She called me a murderer and I lost my temper', O'Rourke

156 Long Reddings Lane, Britwell.

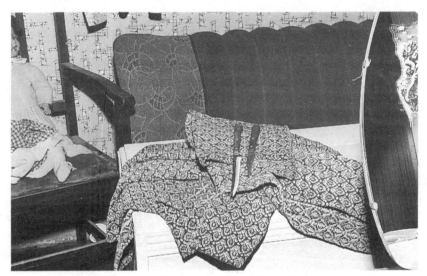

Knives used in the attack on Florrie Regan.

answered and Parris, having some knowledge of his volatility, could believe it.

As he left the cells Parris paused and offered his client some words of advice, 'You had better be careful, even the luck of the Irish will not run to a third time.'

O'Rourke left to serve time at Dartmoor. Eventually, by earning full remission he was released in the Summer of 1958. Florrie was left to bring up a young family by herself but her plight was highlighted in the Sunday newspapers and gifts of clothing and money poured in and she left Yorkshire for London where she was joined by O'Rourke who, having been divorced by his legal wife, was now able to marry her. On leaving prison O'Rourke decided to change his name in an effort to put his past misdeeds behind him once more. He now faced the future as Anthony Regan!

After living for some time in cramped conditions, the Regan family moved to a London Council overspill estate near Slough.

'A garden of my own and flowers. I can't believe it,' Florrie excitedly told John Parris with whom she still kept in touch. But if Regan though that just by changing his name he would change his fortune he was mistaken, for he fell foul of the law again, this time for theft. He even attempted to cash in on his notoriety by boasting to a magazine how he had killed Tom Pickering and Rose Harper.

Such is the power of love that Florrie forgave him and welcomed him into their new home at 156 Long Reddings Lane, Britwell.

Tensions grew between them however, as so often happens when couples move to a new district, and to the local Police the Regans were just one of a number to whom they were called on a fairly regular basis on the estate and which they termed as 'domestic disputes' with an appropriate entry in the Station Occurrence Book.

Things came to such a pass that Joan, Florrie's eldest daughter, moved out of the house and went to live with a friend. Regan became more and more sullen and took to carrying a knife about with him all the time. Florrie confessed to Parris that he frightened her. Parris advised her that if she felt threatened in any way she could leave him but she would not.

On the morning of Saturday, 24th March 1962 things seemed calm enough as Mrs Regan went out shopping. She was wearing a mauve coat and carried a handbag. About mid-day Regan was seen at the house alone and when Joan called he told her that Florrie was still out getting the rest of the shopping. Joan left but returned later and again asked for her mother. Regan informed her that Florrie had come back to the house shortly after Joan's departure but had left virtually straight away and that she was now staying with a Sister of the Church Army in London.

Joan asked her step-father if he would like her to stay at home and tidy up the house ready for her mother returning. Regan agreed to this and whilst she was busy engaged in cleaning Joan telephoned the Church Army Sister enquiring about her mother. She received the rather startling reply that the Sister knew nothing at all about Florrie's whereabouts. Joan

The bed that Detective Chief Inspector Keenan and Detective Sergeant Chambers searched.

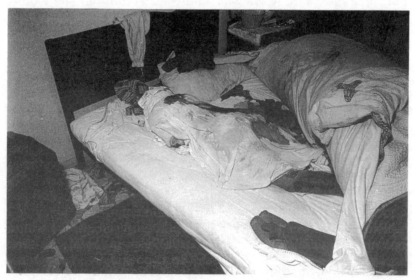

The gruesome sight that the two detectives saw.

Wardrobe in bedroom.

Interior of wardrobe showing stain.

taxed Regan about this and he suggested that she must have gone to stay with her parents in Stockton on Tees.

Joan left the house for a hairdressing appointment and on her return Regan announced that she had just missed her mother. 'Guess where she has been?'

'Stockton?' suggested Joan.

'Yes,' answered Regan, 'she is coming back on Tuesday.'

When Florrie did not turn up on Tuesday Joan left and stayed with a friend.

Florrie was reported as a missing person and from time to time the Police called at the house to see if there was any more information on where she might be. Regan told them of various places she might have gone to and these were all dutifully followed up but to no avail and Florrie could not be traced.

During the next few months a Child Care Officer visited 156 Long Reddings Lane, concerned for the welfare of the other children but had great difficulty in catching Regan at home. Eventually he managed to obtain a signature from Regan consenting to having the children taken into care. But when arrangements were made to collect them Regan made various excuses for not handing them over. They were in Newcastle with relatives; he found it difficult to part with them or he just wanted them over the weekend.

On Saturday 23rd June, Joan came to the house once more. There was no-one in and she was idly looking around when she discovered that her mother and step-father's bedroom door was locked. Curious, Joan popped next door and asked a neighbour if she could borrow her bedroom door key on the off-chance that it fitted her mother's lock. It did and Joan entered the room. At first it was difficult to see anything as the curtains were drawn, but as her eyes adjusted to the gloom she noticed her mother's mauve coat, handbag and a number of shoes lying on top of the bed. But above all there was an overpowering smell that made her want to be sick.

Joan retreated, now thoroughly alarmed and worried by the continuous absence of her mother. After handing the key back she went to Slough and reported these strange facts to the Police.

It was lunchtime and there were a number of CID officers

about and she was passed over to Detective Sergeant (later Chief Inspector) Blackney Chambers. He listened intently to what she told him, gently questioning her and going over her story until he was quite satisfied that it warranted more decisive Police action than it had already received.

Sergeant Chambers conferred with Detective Inspector Henry Keenan who agreed that 156 Long Reddings Lane ought to be visited. Accordingly the two detectives drove out to the address and knocked on the front door. Regan was still not at home and an entry was therefore effected by way of a pane of broken glass in the door, adjacent to the lock. The two CID men entered the still house and slowly, quietly, talking to each other in hushed tones they made their way upstairs in the direction of the locked bedroom door. Placing the key, which they had borrowed from the long-suffering neighbour, in the lock, Sergeant Chambers turned it and gradually opened the door and peered in. He too found it difficult to see anything at first owing to the drawn curtains but his nostrils were assailed by the nauseous smell. The eyes of both detectives now focussed on the bed which, in addition to having Mrs Regan's coat, handbag and shoes on it was piled high with clothing, bedding and a mattress.

Suspecting the worst Inspector Keenan and Sergeant Chambers gingerly removed the articles on the bed until finally they came upon the body of a woman in an advanced state of decomposition. The two policemen gazed down at the pathetic remains and withdrew from the bedroom of horror and went downstairs while they pondered their course of action.

As they discussed their next move, they saw Regan walking along the street towards the house with his dog. Sergeant Chambers stood behind the front door whilst Inspector Keenan positioned himself behind another door. The key in the lock turned and the front door opened. The dog bounded in and went straight to the kitchen. As Regan entered, hands grabbed him in a vice-like grip and propelled him into the front room where he was informed that he was being arrested on suspicion of murder and was then conveyed to Slough Police Station. The usual arrangements were made for uniformed Police Officers to guard the house and its horrific contents and one, PC Stanley

Swan, who was detailed for this unenviable duty, still remembers having to eat his sandwiches in the same room where the body of the late Mrs Regan reposed.

Regan was already thinking ahead for he told the officers, 'When I was away she had a man sleeping with her. When I came back she went to live at Cippenham (a suburb of Slough). We had an argument upstairs. She picked up a knife and there was a struggle. I gave her a wound in the chest. I put a first aid dressing on it and left her there hoping she would come round but she didn't. It happened eight to twelve weeks before.'

Regan admitted that he had initially put the body of his wife in the wardrobe in their bedroom but as Florrie's body began to decompose he had moved it to the bed and piled clothing and bedding on top in a vain attempt to disguise the smell.

Professor Camps, the noted Home Office pathologist, performed the post mortem on the body of Florrie, which was identified by fingerprints, as hers had been taken by the Police some years before when she had been arrested for a minor offence. Professor Camps found two wounds in the chest – one was two to two-and-a-half inches long, the other about two inches which had punctured the heart and the lung. Death, he estimated, would have occurred in three to five minutes.

When Regan appeared at Number One Court at the Old Bailey in September, Professor Camps was closely questioned to see if the wounds he had described could have been caused the way Regan had suggested. By producing photographs and showing the angle of entry Camps was able to disprove Regan's allegation.

Regan finally went into the witness box and made an effort to try and charm the jury for a third time on a murder charge. He was handed the knife which had killed his wife and asked to explain the events on that Spring day earlier in the year. On March 24th, he related, Florrie had come back from doing the shopping and he had made her a cup of tea which she had drunk. She had then started arguing with him over his not going shopping with her. He had gone upstairs to the toilet and she had gone to the bedroom. When he had emerged from the toilet he had seen her changing her clothes, she already had her skirt and blouse off. He had asked her where she was going and she had replied, 'To London,' and had mentioned the name of a male friend. Regan went on, 'She'd had intercourse with him, she told me. I'd quarrelled with her about him and forgiven her. I asked her frequently to forget about him. When she said she was going I said, "He's been the cause of all the trouble. Why don't you forget him?" She said, "I'll make sure you don't stop me,' in a bad tempered voice. She picked up the knife, which she used to peel apples, from the set of drawers near the bed. She was standing by the side of the bed. I was standing on the same side . . . she picked it up and turned round to stick it in me. I grabbed her wrists. I told her not to be daft. I held both her wrists and she was trying to get free. When she was hysterical she was strong. I was trying to get the knife from her. She had her hands up and then I suppose I must have slipped and she went stiff in my arms.'

It was at this point that Mr Mervyn Griffith-Jones, for the prosecution, interrupted Regan and instructed him to stop waving the knife about and he was handed a rubber one instead.

Regan continued with his story. 'She went stiff and then fell on the bed. I fell on top of her. I thought the mat had slipped away. I didn't know the knife had gone into her chest. When I got off her she didn't move. She was stiff. When I turned her over I saw blood, the knife was lying in her chest. I ran to the bathroom and got a First-Aid dressing and put it on where the blood was. I didn't know there was more than one injury. I wrapped the bandage around her arm to stop it slipping. I felt panic and worry. She didn't move or say anything. About ten minutes after putting the bandage on I realised she was dead.'

When Griffith-Jones rose to cross-examine Regan he asked him to demonstrate on a Prison Officer how the struggle had taken place.

After Regan had showed how his version of the attack had occurred Griffith-Jones asked why, if he had not meant Florrie to die, he had not done something about it.

'I just panicked,' answered Regan.

'Why did you take the knife downstairs and wash it? You objected to the children seeing the knife?' suggested Counsel.

'Yes, it didn't look a nice thing for the kiddies to see,' was the weak response.

'You wife's body wasn't a nice thing for them to see was it?' Mr Griffith-Jones queried.

'I covered it up. It was natural to wash the knife.'

'Is it a natural thing to do nothing, cover her up with bedclothes, then wash the knife and put it back into daily use?'

Regan's reply was a barely audible, 'No.'

There was a pause while the Jury were allowed to take that in.

The Police, in their thorough search of the Regan's house, had found a diary which Regan had kept, including an entry some days after the date of the killing.

Mr Griffith-Jones now held it up for all to see and addressed Regan once more. 'In the diary you wrote, "I loved my wife but also loved her daughter, Joan". Why?'

'Because the wife seemed to think I loved the younger children more than I loved Joan.'

'But your wife would have been dead ten days when that was written. What was the point? What did you mean?'

'I've told you.'

'Or is the truth that you quite deliberately killed your wife . . .'

'No sir.'

'. . . and that at sometime you decided to confess and that the reason you killed your wife was because you loved your step-daughter?'

'No sir.'

There was a stillness as the questioning of Regan finished and he made the long walk back to the box.

Both Counsel summed up, with Mr Griffith-Jones contending that the entry in the diary, '. . . I loved my wife but I also loved her daughter', proved that Regan had a deeper, more sinister reason for killing his wife.

After three and a half hours' deliberation the Jury returned and to a hushed Court the foreman announced that they found Regan guilty of the murder of Florrie. Mr Justice Roskill turned from the Jury to the prisoner. 'The Jury, who knew nothing of your record, have found a just and true verdict. They did not know that ten years ago you were sent to prison for ten years for manslaughter and that this is the second human being you have killed by violence.' He then sentenced Regan to life imprisonment and he was swiftly taken below by the Prison Officers.

Allowing that the Judge had miscounted the number of people who had died by Regan's hand, Justice had at last caught up with him.

The Armistice Day Murder

R.A.F. Halton, Wendover 1967

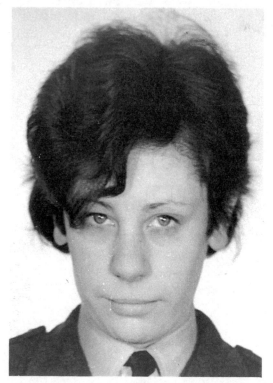

Rita Ellis.

On a dark, dank November evening in 1967, when most people had decided to settle down in front of their television sets to watch the Val Doonican Show and The Festival of remembrance on BBC1, Aircraftwoman Rita Irene Ellis was getting ready to go out. Nineteen year old Rita had only served in the WRAF a few months, having done her basic training in Lincolnshire before being posted to RAF Halton, near Wendover, as a cook just two months previously. This evening she was quite excited as she was baby-sitting for a high-ranking RAF officer, Wing Commander Watson and his wife. The usual baby-sitter was away and a WRAF Corporal had arranged that Rita would take her place. As she did not know what the Wing Commander looked like he had told her that he would collect her, from outside the block where she lived, in his large car and take her to his house about a mile from the Camp to look after his children while he and his wife went out for the night. This was the first time she had performed this job and she did not want to be late. A friend, Sylvia Banks, went to Rita's room and while she was there Rita went to the window and looked out to see if the car had arrived. To Sylvia Banks, Rita was a quiet girl who did not smoke or drink and seemed to spend most of her time reading or watching television.

As the appointed time drew near, Rita made her way out of the brightness of the block and peered into the gloom. She

Rita Ellis' pass – to death.

noticed a large car being slowly driven in her direction. The driver, seeing her, pulled over, opened the door and Rita got in. The car then sped off.

Wing Commander Watson was a few minutes late as he drove his car onto the RAF Camp and up to Block 7 where he had arranged to rendezvous with Rita Ellis. He stopped his car and waited. When, after five minutes, she had not appeared he asked two passing WRAF girls to go into the block and look for her. When they returned and told him they could not find her the Wing Commander, somewhat puzzled, drove home, picked up his wife and returned to the RAF Camp to see if Rita was by now outside Block 7. She was not there and Mrs Vivienne Watson went into the WRAF Quarters and found Rita's room but it was empty, neither could she find anyone who had seen Rita recently. After waiting for about an hour and as the young Aircraftwoman showed no sign of turning up, Wing Commander Watson and his wife decided to drive off.

The next morning as the nation prepared to remember the fallen of two World Wars and numerous other conflicts at ceremonies all over the country, Flight Sergeant Arthur Jones was exercising his dog through the RAF Camp, when it wandered off into the woodland at the rear of a coal-dump. Suddenly, he saw his dog bound upwards and sideways as though something had startled it. Wandering over to where his dog now stood, the Flight Sergeant saw what he thought was a dummy or a guy but which on closer inspection he realised was the body of a young girl. It now became abundantly clear why Rita Ellis had failed to keep her appointment with the Wing Commander the previous evening. For there under a covering of leaves and bracken lay the partly-clothed body of the WRAF girl. She had been beaten, sexually assaulted and strangled and her body dumped where it had been found at 10.30am on Sunday.

Detective Sergeant William Baker from the Buckinghamshire Constabulary Headquarters at Aylesbury was one of the first on the scene. He saw that the body had been almost completely covered over by bracken. He also noticed that the dead girl's pants were around her neck forming a ligature, whilst other items of her clothing were on tree branches and brambles nearby.

Scene of the murder of Rita Ellis at R.A.F. Halton

The body of Rita Ellis.

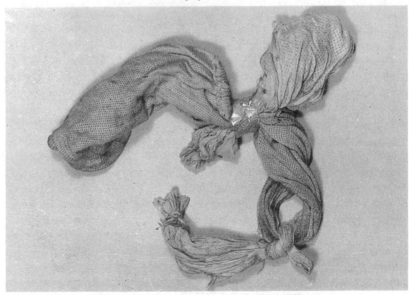

The clothing used to strangle Rita Ellis.

An Incident Room was quickly set up by Detective Inspector (later Detective Superintendent) Philip Fairweather and Detective Sergeant (later Detective Chief Superintendent) Keith Milner, the officer who had proved his organisational ability when he had been the Exhibits Officer for the Great Train Robbery some four years before.

Detective Chief Inspector John Schofield (later Superintendent) of the Regional Crime Squad was informed and, perceiving that a large number of detectives would be needed at least for the initial investigation, decided to call on virtually the whole of the central area of No.5 District RCS. Among the first to attend were Detective Constables Terry Lee and Peter Walker of Aylesbury (both later Detective Sergeants) and all experienced in investigating major crimes.

Uniform Police Officers were also called upon as well and in those days, before personal radios were issued, they had to be whisked away by cars and vans from the Remembrance Day Parades they were attending in towns and villages in the locality.

One of the first duties was to preserve the area where the body of Rita Ellis had been found in order that the pathologist and scenes of crime officers could do their essential work. It did not help when, a few minutes later, an RAF Sergeant commenced to walk over the scene of the murder. When spoken to by the Constable on guard, the NCO replied that he usually walked in this direction and nothing and no-one was going to stop him now. Detective Sergeant Milner's feelings when he heard of this, despite all his precautions, can be imagined.

Professor Keith Simpson, the eminent pathologist, attended, gently loosened the pants from around the neck of the dead girl and could see the marks where they had been tightened. A cardigan, which he found near her mouth, looked as though it had been used to muffle any screams she might have uttered, whilst bruises on her body showed that she had put up a strong fight against her attacker. Professor Simpson also saw that she had been sexually assaulted.

It was decided to call in Scotland Yard and Detective Superintendent Evans was sent down and was briefed on the circumstances of the murder. He hoped that it would be cleared up in as short a time as possible as he informed the local Police that he was retiring in a few weeks' time. If it were not, then he would be handing over to another Metropolitan Police Officer.

As the murder occurred on an RAF Camp, the Royal Air Force Special Investigation Branch, who are trained in carrying out criminal enquiries, assisted the civilian Police. With the large number of personnel on the camp they were reinforced by RAF Police. This initially caused some problems as any minor breaches of the Royal Air Force's Discipline Code that might have been committed by an Airman and mentioned to the investigating officers, would immediately be noted by the RAF Police. For example, great efforts were being made to trace and if possible eliminate any cars that were about on the night of the murder. However if an Airman admitted that he owned and kept a car on the RAF Camp he was told straightaway that he had committed an offence against Discipline Regulations. Consequently the Airmen were not saying too much at all. This was eventually pointed out and the RAF Police were told to close an eye to minor infractions in an effort to get the servicemen to 'open up'.

Strenuous efforts were made to contact and interview, not only all the personnel on the Camp but also others who were used to driving through – there is a main road bisecting Halton Camp, leading from Wendover to Tring. Also any contacts that Rita Ellis may have had at the RAF Station in Lincolnshire where she had performed her basic training were also traced. In all, over two thousand Servicemen and women and six hundred and seventy civilians working in the camp were seen. Enquiries were made at three hundred other camps and four and a half thousand people living in the locality were interviewed. Eventually five and a half thousand statements were taken and over eight thousand questionnaires completed.

All types of cars were traced and the usual suspects seen and interviewed as to their whereabouts on the night of the murder. The BBC were even asked to supply a copy of the script used in the Val Doonican Show to check against the alibis used by various persons.

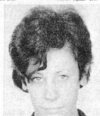

Newspaper coverage of murder hunt.

Superintendent Evans, as mentioned, retired and was replaced by Detective Superintendent (later Commander) Roy Yorke, who had to go through all the statements taken by the investigating teams in order to brief himself on the current state of the enquiry.

After several weeks, as damp and foggy Autumn became cold and frosty Winter the investigation dragged on, becoming a round of routine enquiries by a smaller team of Officers, all trying desperately to uncover some clue that might lead to the discovery of the murderer. Each day, 'actions' were handed out to various detectives that morning to visit persons who might provide that one glimmer of light in a seemingly inpenetrable mystery. Each night they would return to the Incident Room and hand over any statements they had taken for the perusal of Sergeant Milner, Inspector Fairweather and Superintendent Yorke. The long, hard, grinding slog of a major enquiry went on.

Christmas came and went and a New Year approached but still there was no breakthrough in the search for Rita's killer.

It seemed as though it might have come when, in the early evening of Thursday, 28th December, a student nurse alighted from a bus at Tring, a small market town only a few miles from RAF Halton, and started walking towards her friend's house in Little Tring, a nearby hamlet. As she walked down the quiet country lane she became aware of a man walking ahead of her. He turned and spoke to her and then suddenly grabbed her and took her into a field where he struck her with an object and seriously sexually assaulted her. Although she screamed out it was to no avail as there was no one to hear. He left her unconscious, lying in the field, and made off. When she recovered consciousness, she struggled to a farm close by and was taken to the nearest hospital and detained.

This being a different Police area, initially the Hertfordshire Constabulary investigated the matter but with the knowledge that this was a similar type of attack to the one upon Rita Ellis, although this time not fatal, the murder was kept in mind and teams from the Regional Crime Squad were sent to assist.

A description of the young woman's attacker was obtained; he was described as between 25–30 years, slim to medium

Funeral of Rita Ellis.

build, gaunt features, long thin face, hollow cheeks and 'slit' eyes with a 'puffiness' above and below them. He had a local accent and had been wearing a light grey or green trilby hat with the brim pulled forward, a dark coloured overcoat and a tartan or maroon scarf and black leather gloves.

Again, despite prodigious efforts by the Police, the case was unresolved and, as can be imagined, there was an undercurrent of fear running through this part of Buckinghamshire and Hertfordshire. This was not helped when, just over a month later a fifteen year old girl in a village in the locality said that when she had been walking down a country lane just after midnight she had been accosted by a man, similar in description to the one who had so violently attacked the student nurse. Again, despite thorough Police investigations the matter was never satisfactorily cleared up.

A year went by and on the anniversary of the murder a team of Police Officers led by Chief Inspector Schofield went back to the scene and questioned all persons they saw in the vicinity to ascertain if they had been in the area around the time that Rita had been murdered. Unfortunately no good results came of these endeavours.

A rather strange incident occurred shortly after this when a seventeen year old girl complained that she had been sexually assaulted by a man. She had met him after she had lost her job and run away to avoid being sent back to a Children's Home. He had offered her accommodation in his caravan which he kept in a scrap metal yard at Halton near the RAF Camp and where he had worked since October 1967. Although he was several years older than her, she had accepted. She had stayed for several days and alleged that on two of the nights he had committed serious sexual assaults on her. During the time she had remained with him he repeatedly mentioned that an unsolved murder had taken place only a short distance from where he lived in the caravan and he even offered to take her there during the night. An offer she had declined.

The man was brought in and questioned about this and the Rita Ellis murder and it transpired that he had a car which he had kept hidden since the killing. Although Forensic experts carefully examined it, it was by now too late to gather anything useful from the vehicle.

The man of course denied not only the offences against the seventeen year old but naturally enough also any involvement in the Rita Ellis case and although tried at the Assizes was acquitted on the indecency counts.

How he had been overlooked in the initial Police Investigation remains for ever a matter of conjecture.

The murder of young Rita Ellis was never solved and remains a mystery to this day.

The ALTER EGO MURDER

Amersham 1972

In the Summer of 1972 Pauline Allison Stevens stood on the very threshold of a promising life with everything to look forward to. She was young, nineteen years old, a Sunday School teacher and she was hoping to go eventually to a teachers' training college in London. The future looked bright for a girl who could lead a fulfilling life and be an asset not only to herself and those who knew her but to the community in general. Her parents ran the sub-post office in Amersham Old Town and on the afternoon of Saturday 3rd June they took Pauline with them to Windsor where the recently deceased Duke of Windsor was lying in state. On their return to Amersham Mr and Mrs Stevens decided to go on a family visit and asked if Pauline wanted to come along. She declined, saying that she wished to revise for her A Level examination which she was to take soon at High Wycombe College where she was studying English, biology, zoology and maths. Mr and Mrs Stevens left her and drove off. It was only a few minutes after her parents had gone that Pauline decided to go out herself, perhaps to clear her mind before revising. She changed her clothes, left her books open on a table, the lights on and the gas fire burning. It was a fatal decision.

A few minutes later a couple who were driving along School Lane, which runs to the rear of Amersham Old Town saw a body illuminated in the headlights of their car. Thinking it was the casualty of a 'hit and run' accident they drove on and contacted the local Police. A few seconds later another motorist travelling along the same stretch of road noticed a man moving a body from the road towards the bushes at the side. As the lights of the car picked him out he took fright at being disturbed and ran off, leaving the body lying on the damp earth. This incident was also reported to the Police. Asked to return to the scene to await the arrival of the police, the first motorist did so. When he reached the spot he saw that the body had disappeared! He noticed blood in the road however and then noticed a man walking towards him. The motorist saw the body now lying in the gateway to a house. The stranger threw an object into the hedge, had a short, obscene conversation with the motorist then left, just as the Police arrived. When the first Officers arrived on the scene they expected to find a victim of some reckless or dangerous driving. Instead, a quick look was enough to satisfy them they they had come across someone who had been subjected to a savage and brutal attack. It did not take long to establish that the body was that of Pauline Stevens and a more thorough examination revealed that she had been repeatedly stabbed in her throat and back. There was also a long slash under her jaw.

Immediately a murder investigation commenced. Placed in charge was Detective Superintendent Joe Coffey of the Thames Valley Constabulary, a quietly spoken Irishman, well used to handling murder enquiries and ably assisted by Chief Inspector Jim Buckle. As usual a large team of Police Officers, including local and Regional Crime Squad detectives descended on the nearest Police Station at Amersham where an Incident Room was quickly set up. Here they were given a briefing by Superintendent Coffey and handed various 'actions' to complete. At first there seemed very little to go on. The fact that the murderer had quite likely been seen shortly after committing this atrocious crime was negated somewhat by the fact that only a vague description could be given by the motorists and Police Officers who had seen him. It was quite dark, in an unlit lane on an inclement night. The description given was of a man about five foot eight or nine inches with dark hair partially covering his ears and of stocky build. An artist's impression of the suspect was handed out to various newspapers asking the public for assistance in tracing the man.

As soon as practicable a very thorough search of the scene of the murder was undertaken under the direction of Detective Inspector John White, one of the most capable Scene of Crime Officers in the Police at that time. Pauline's shoes were discovered a short distance from her body though whether they had been taken off or had more likely come off during the course of the struggle was not at this stage known. Inspector White sent the shoes and Pauline's other clothing including a

Pauline Alison Stevens' newspaper coverage of murder hunt.

brown tapestry coat, brown skirt and beige floral shirt to the Atomic Research Establishment at Harwell where a new treatment was used. The item of clothing to be examined was interlaid with X-ray film and the whole article was bombarded with radio-active rays. This test had to be performed within a few short hours of the commission of a crime and any clothing found in the open air was not really suitable as damp adversely affected the process. It could be seen quite clearly on the X-ray negative where an arm had been forcibly gripped through the shirt sleeve. The second test which Inspector White asked to be carried out was on the pair of shoes belonging to Pauline. Here, the treatment involved the use of gold or silver, depending on the colour of the material on which it was being tested and again subjected to radioactivity in an effort to raise any hidden finger impressions. Unfortunately, despite the efforts of the scientists, nothing of consequence was revealed. There was one item of Pauline's clothing that could not be found where she had been murdered however; her knickers.

One interesting discovery found in the thorough Police search of the area near the murder was a rough bivouac-type shelter built of corrugated iron sheeting in a spinney half a mile from the scene of the murder. Every item found in this shelter

The shack discovered by police during the hunt.

was minutely examined as it was thought at the time that this could have been where the murderer had been living rough.

The teams of detectives were busy on house to house enquiries as well as interviewing students at High Wycombe College, taking statements from everyone they thought might just possibly have some useful information to impart. In the first twenty-four hours of the investigation over one thousand pages of statements were taken, all of which were handed in to the staff back at the Incident Room to be studied carefully for any hint of the identity of the killer.

The murder attracted, as most do that are not cleared up immediately, the usual 'cranks' who pester the Police with their weird theories on how the case could be solved. One woman continually telephoned the Police Station wishing to speak to Superintendent Coffey. She invited him to take part in a 'hand-hold experience' around a table at her home in an effort to find the answer to the crime. Mr Coffey adroitly passed her over to a Policewoman.

The Incident Room staff were, day after day, carefully reading every statement in an effort to glean something positive but as they went through this long slow process nothing much that appeared to be of any assistance to the investigation came out. Except for one small matter mentioned by a lady living at Stanley Hill, Amersham. She had noticed, on Saturday afternoon, a man park his car on part of the grass verge opposite her house and commence cleaning it out. At the time he was doing this chore she had seen a dog in the car. Thinking this was rather a cheeky thing to do she had taken the number of the car and had reported the matter to the Police. This had been handed into the Incident Room and it had been 'actioned' out to a detective. The car, of course had long since gone from the grass verge but a search of the area where the car had been parked revealed that a pair of knickers had been left behind! These were later identified as belonging to Pauline. At last there was something to go on. A detailed description of the car was obtained from the witness and this was checked against the registration number that she had written down. Unfortunately they did not tally. The car number, as so often happens, had been taken incorrectly.

The description of the car was circulated as a matter of course and a member of the public came forward stating that a man driving a similar car had called at an all night service station and had cleaned himself up in the gentlemen's washroom in the middle of the night, after the murder had taken place. Later that night the same car had been noticed being driven erratically in Uxbridge and had been approached by Police Officers. On checking the driver, who produced a birth certificate in the name of Clive Graham Maskell, he gave the Policeman an address in Cornwall and the Officer, not having any knowledge of the murder, allowed Maskell to continue on his way.

Meanwhile the Police now had to check the combination of numbers in an effort to match them up with the car. In 1972 this had to be done manually as all motor vehicles were registered with the various County and County Borough Councils. Placing them on a central computer was still some years away. When a number was found that appeared to tie in with the make of the car detectives went quickly round to the owner only to find that he had sold it a few days beforehand to a Clive Graham Maskell.

The Police called at the Cornish address, where they spoke to Maskell's stepfather who informed the Detectives that his son no longer lived with him, having left a few days previously, with his dog to which he was quite attached, to live in London. At first sight Maskell's move to the capital appeared to be an almost insuperable problem for he could be virtually swallowed up in the myriad of streets and houses abounding there but Maskell's stepfather then added that he had received a letter from him from an address in North London. He was sure it was from his stepson although he had signed it, for some unaccountable reason, with the name 'Ysabel'. This news was immediately relayed to Superintendent Coffey who requested the Flying Squad to call at the address, in Mora Road NW2, and if Maskell were residing there, to arrest him on suspicion of Pauline's murder.

There was one more confusing thing. Why was Maskell calling himself by the name 'Ysabel'? No one seemed to have the faintest notion until Mr Coffey mentioned it at one of the evening de-briefings. A detective suggested that it might be a subject from a popular novelist – J T Edson – who wrote prolifically about the American West. One of the characters written about was a half-breed Indian who violently dispatched a number of his enemies by knifing them in the back. His name was Loncey Dalton Ysabel and the manner of killing was similar to the way in which Pauline had been murdered. Superintendent Coffey made a mental note to expand his reading in the future.

A message was received from the Flying Squad. They had visited the flat only to find that Maskell was out, though he had left his dog behind. They had questioned the landlord who thought that his lodger had merely gone out looking for work. He had informed the detectives that his new lodger had only recently arrived asking for lodgings which he had provided. The only odd thing about him was that he had used a funny name on his arrival at her house. Superintendent Coffey asked them to remain at the address until Maskell, or 'Ysabel' as he preferred to be called, returned.

Although there was still plenty of work to keep the Incident Room busy there was now a sense of expectancy in the air as they waited for the call from London. Although it seemed an age it was not long before the Flying Squad rang again to say that they had arrested Maskell and had taken him to Cannon Row Police Station. They had, most interestingly, found a Bowie knife in his possession but Maskell vehemently denied all knowledge of the murder of Pauline Stevens. Immediately Superintendent Coffey, accompanied by Chief Inspector Buckle and Inspector White travelled post haste to Cannon Row Police Station; Inspector White took the knife and then made his way to the house in Mora Road, where the suspect had been detained. Maskell was brought to the interview room where he was confronted by the two senior Police Officers. He refused to acknowledge his name and he insisted on being addressed as 'Ysabel'. Gently they talked to him but for a long time 'Ysabel' refused to speak or even look at the detectives. It was only when Superintendent Coffey mentioned the care of 'Ysabel's' dog that any sort of response was elicited from him. He looked up into Joe Coffey's eyes and asked if he really meant what he said, adding that if the Superintendent was straight about looking after his dog he would tell everything he knew. When Mr Coffey assured 'Ysabel' that his dog would be cared for, the strange young man made a detailed statement which Chief Inspector Buckle took down.

Meanwhile, Detective Inspector White had been painstakingly going through 'Ysabel's' room at Mora Road. He found some paper on which Maskell had repeatedly practised writing the name 'Ysabel'. Nearby were some J T Edson novels about the character Loncey Dalton Ysabel. Most importantly was discovered a waistcoat of Maskell/'Ysabel' on which were some bloodstains. These were later identified as being of the same group as Pauline Stevens. There were also more bloodstains in his car on the front of the driving seat. Taken to Amersham Police Station Maskell/'Ysabel' was placed on an identification parade and was picked out by several witnesses as being at the scene of the murder.

'Ysabel' was charged with the murder of Pauline Stevens and in November, 1972 he appeared at Reading Crown Court where he pleaded not guilty to the murder of Pauline Stevens but guilty to manslaughter by reason of diminished responsibility. The Court was told that 'Ysabel' had joined the Royal Navy at fifteen but had been discharged when it was found that he was suffering from schizophrenia. In June 1972 he had made his way to the Amersham area and had, on the 3rd, bought a car which had continually broken down throughout the afternoon and evening. He became fed up and had walked along to School Lane where he saw Pauline out for her stroll. He had walked up behind her and had then viciously attached her, stabbing her in the neck and kidneys. He had been arrested after the most intensive Police enquiries one week after the commission of the murder.

A senior Medical Officer who had made reports on the condition of the prisoner and who was asked if he was a danger to the public, replied, 'Yes. I think he is, particularly to women. A similar situation could arise again. he might approach a woman and be rejected or scorned by her and attack her.'

Mr Justice Eveleigh, the judge, therefore committed this highly dangerous young man to Broadmoor under an Indefinite Restriction Order.

EXECUTION in the FOREST

Salcey Forest 1983

Part One

All that now remains of the vast wooded area that for centuries covered North Buckinghamshire and South Northamptonshire are Whittlewood Forest, Yardley Chase and Salcey Forest. These were once the exclusive privilege of the Kings and the nobility of this country to hunt over, to the exclusion of the common people. Now, anyone can visit and walk through the acres of woodland in this quiet and still to some extent remote part of the countryside.

So it was on Sunday, April 3rd 1983, Easter Day, that a family from Leighton Buzzard were out walking in Salcey Forest. These were the first real stirrings of Spring, although the days were still inclined to be chilly, but people were determined to go out whatever the weather after the long winter months. However, as the teenage son and his friend were looking around they came across a sight which sent a shudder down their spines and made them set off at once to inform the Police.

PC David Burton, stationed at Newport Pagnell, received the call and drove the few miles to the forest where he met the two rather excited teenagers. they took him to the spot where they had made their gruesome discovery. There, in the dense undergrowth, PC Burton saw what at first sight appeared to be just a pile of discarded clothing but which on closer examination he noticed had bones poking through. Looking around he also noticed that a few yards away were two skulls.

Realising that he was confronting something even more sinister than an ordinary sudden death PC Burton summoned assistance and a team of uniform Police and detectives descended on the scene, supervised by Detective Superintendent Ken Diccox of the Thames Valley Police who had been called out from an enjoyable gathering with friends. It was, after some high level and lengthy discussions, ascertained that the bones lay within the Buckinghamshire border.

It appeared that the bodies, or skeletons as they had now been reduced to, had been in the forest for some considerable time. They were all the remains that were left of a man and a woman and from a cursory examination it was obvious that the male had been subjected to a brutal attack, although whether the wounds had been caused by an axe or hatchet or something similar was not discernible at this stage; all that could be said was that the horrific injuries had not been caused by a shotgun blast.

Detective Superintendent Ken Diccox – leader of the team that solved the murders in Salcey Forest.

With the ravages of time and the depredations performed by the animals in the forest, identification of the two deceased was going to be difficult and at first only a general description could be given to the media, together with photographs of the clothes they had been wearing. Pictures were published in the local papers including those of a bracelet worn by the man bearing the name DAVE and a ring worn by the woman. One of the patches found on one item of clothing read, 'CB'ers are great lovers', and the Police were apparently inundated with calls from CB radio enthusiasts who thought they knew who the victims were.

Within a few days a Mrs Cox from Wellingborough came forward and suggested that the man might be her stepson David John Cox aged twenty-three years who lived at a Northampton address with his common-law wife Deborah (or Debbie) Jayne Fallon, aged nineteen years. She had last seen David on Father's Day the previous year when he had visited

Debbie Fallon and David Cox – the victims in the forest.

her and Mr Cox. Her husband, she told the Police, had given David a T-shirt similar to that shown in the newspapers. Neither she nor the parents of Debbie had reported them missing as they were always talking about going up to London to live and it was assumed that that is what they had done. The dental records for the couple were checked and by the 17th April the identification was complete.

Superintendent Diccox directed his detectives to find out all they could about Cox and Fallon, even to what they had eaten on their last day.

It transpired that David Cox had been adopted by Mr and Mrs Cox as they could have no children of their own and by 1982 David had become a resident at Thorplands Probation Hostel, Northampton. Debbie Fallon had gone there as she was unable to find employment and she and David had signed up to perform voluntary work.

It was to this Hostel that a Stephen John Parkinson, aged twenty-one, had gone. He had been born in Aden, his father serving in the Royal Air Force at the time. He had, however, spent most of his life in Market Deeping but he had left his parents' home when he was seventeen and had drifted from job to job ending up as a dustman in Peterborough. He was also reputed to have used drugs. He had an interest in CB radio which he shared with another visitor to the Hostel, Michael Dennis Bardell, aged thirty.

Bardell had a keen pre-occupation with the occult and had for some years wanted to form a chapter of the Hell's Angels in Northampton. In 1981 he had organised a group called Lucifer's Outlaws of which he was the head and Parkinson was his right-hand man and responsible for looking after the group's weaponry.

About this time Bardell had struck up a friendship with a woman called Sue Turner who had for a short time left her husband and gone to live with Bardell, but by 1982 she had informed Bardell that she could no longer live with him

Stephen John Parkinson – who aided in the execution of Cox and Fallon and the attempted murder of Ian Turner.

and was returning to her husband. Bardell had been very angry at hearing this and had encountered the Turners one evening and, brandishing a machette, had threatened to commit some serious bodily harm to Ian Turner. He was only prevented from doing so by Sue intervening on her husband's behalf.

Sue Turner later telephoned Bardell and admitted that she still loved him. Bardell told her that he had received a call from a group of Hell's Angels based in London called the Road Rats telling him that they were not satisfied with the Lucifer's Outlaws and wanted three people 'wasted', which she understood to mean killed. When Sue Turner telephoned Bardell on another occasion he told her that 'they' were going to kill Dave Cox and Debbie Fallon that night and that he had to be in London the next day with proof of the killing for the Road Rats. Bardell told Sue that the Road Rats were angry that a woman, Parkinson's girl friend, have revealed where an

Michael Bardell –
an egotist and
ruthless killer

armoury was. She could not understand why the girl friend was not one of the three to die but Bardell said he had made a bargain getting her out of it. Bardell told Sue that if the three were not wasted the Road Rats had intimated that they would come to Northampton and 'do' all of them.

She arranged to meet Bardell in a pub on the outskirts of London, where the Turners were now living, the next day to discuss matters and it was here that Bardell related to her an horrific story.

Parkinson and he had met David Cox and Debbie Fallon in Weston Favell, a suburb of Northampton and had induced the couple to go with them to Salcey Forest on the pretext of looking for some treasure. On their arrival at the forest Parkinson had stabbed Cox but had not killed him. He, Bardell, had then taken the knife from Parkinson and had 'finished Cox off'. Debbie, who had been tied to a tree pleaded for her life but Bardell had calmly walked over to her and had broken her neck.

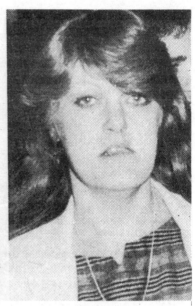

Ian and Sue Turner – she gave vital evidence to the police.

To prove what he had said was true, Bardell produced some photographs of the bodies. They were of poor quality however and he also showed, to Sue, Debbie Fallon's panties which he had removed from her body. Initially, Sue Turner was later to relate, she could not believe what Bardell had told her as he seemed so calm and collected, especially when, mistakenly as it turned out, there were sightings of the couple after the supposed murders. Bardell offered to take her to Salcey Forest and show her the bodies but she declined. Bardell now added that the third person to be killed at the behest of the Road Rats was her husband Ian!

A few days after, Parkinson phoned Turner and arranged a meeting to discuss various matters. As he left, Sue told him to 'Watch out' and not to turn his back on Parkinson for a second. Turner decided to take his dog and two knives with him. The two men drove into the country and got out of the car and walked into a field. Catching Turner momentarily off-guard Parkinson came up behind him and stabbed him in the back.

EXECUTION IN THE FOREST

Turner chased Parkinson and when he caught up with him demanded to know the reason for the sudden and unprovoked attack. Parkinson replied that the Road Rats had told him that he had to be killed. Turner did not believe this as it seemed more likely to him that Bardell had ordered his death. There was a brief struggle but when Turner had started flailing about with his dog lead, Parkinson had decided to quit the field of battle. Turner called his wife, told her what had happened and was taken to Northampton General Hospital for treatment for his wounds.

Bardell had visited him whilst he was at the hospital and had told him to keep his mouth shut and Turner replied that he would keep the Police out of it. Bardell then described to him how he had had to kill Cox and Fallon to save the whole crew but became emotional and had left the hospital room when he had burst out crying.

When he had been discharged from Northampton General Hospital he had seen Bardell, who had told him that both he and Parkinson had had to pay the Road Rats £1,000 because they had failed to kill Turner.

Quite coincidentally, Police Sergeant Ivor Jones of the Northamptonshire Constabulary had interviewed Parkinson over a motoring offence shortly after this affray and being curious as to how Parkinson had received his wounds had asked him to account for them. At first Parkinson said he had been injured because of group of Hell's Angels had taken out a contract to kill him. Sergeant Jones had scoffed at these remarks and had pressed Parkinson further on the matter. Parkinson then said that he had met Ian Turner after putting it over the CB radio that his wife was a slag. 'We knew,' he went on, 'we had to get things sorted out.'

In the absence of any complaint, however, matters could not be proceeded with but Sergeant Jones remembered the incident almost a year later when the bodies in Salcey Forest were found and identified.

Part Two

Superintendent Diccox, although not knowing the whole background to the murders decided that Bardell and Parkinson must be brought in for questioning. Accordingly he ordered that their respective houses should be raided and the two men arrested.

Here, however, he encountered a snag. It was thought that the two men would have firearms with them and might use them on the Police. As both Bardell and Parkinson lived in Northampton, Superintendent Diccox, as a matter of courtesy, informed his opposite number in the Northamptonshire Constabulary of his proposed action and requested the use of the local firearms team to accompany his unarmed officers on the raids. He was informed that the Northamptonshire Constabulary did not possess a tactical firearms unit. Superintendent Diccox replied that it was no great problem as Thames Valley Police had an excellent unit themselves and would be willing and prepared to carry out the work. The response was that the Chief Constable of Northamptonshire would not sanction armed officers from another Police force working in his area!

Therefore, in the early hours of Sunday, April 10th 1983, unarmed Police Officers called at the houses of the the two suspects, Superintendent Diccox and Detective Inspector Peter Cusworth going to the address of Bardell. Believing that both men were 'tooled up', time was of the essence. There could be no polite knocking at the door, informing the men that they were Police Officers investigating a murder and could they please answer a few questions. The front door had to be forced and the men found and rendered harmless, before they could reach for any guns they might have and use them. As Bardell's door was sprung open Inspector Cusworth leapt up the stairs, crashed into the bedroom and discovered that the last thing Bardell had on his mind was reaching for any guns. For there in bed was their man with Sue Turner and another woman. Inspector Cusworth, never at a loss for words and with a fine sense of occasion, took in the whole scene immediately and announced who he was and calmly informed Bardell that he was under arrest on suspicion of murder, adding as an aside that perhaps he and his friends might like to put their clothes on first before accompanying the Officers to the Police Station.

Taken to the nearest Police Station, Bardell was interviewed by Inspector Cusworth. He told the Police Officer that he had talked to Parkinson about forming a chapter of the Hell's Angels. They had designed the 'colours' and had given the chapter a name – 'Lucifer's Outlaws'. They had tried to form an alliance of sorts with the London 'Road Rats' but this 'went sour'. Then, the Road Rats had claimed that because of a mistake committed by the Outlaws, they were going to wipe his chapter out. He had bargained with the Road Rats and had been told that the only way of getting round the threat was to kill three people. Thus it was that Cox and Fallon had been taken to Salcey Forest in June 1982 by himself and Parkinson But it had been Parkinson who had carried out the murders whilst he, horrified, had stood by. Parkinson had stabbed Cox and had then strangled Fallon. Bardell told Inspector Cusworth that Debbie Fallon should, in typical Hell's Angel fashion, have been raped before being strangled but this had not happened as he had 'froze'. After she had been killed he, Bardell, had torn her panties from her body in an effort to make it look as though she had in fact been raped. He had then attempted to take photographs of her but they had not come out very well. He further admitted to having had sexual intercourse with Fallon on several occasions but he denied murdering Cox because he, Cox, had not wanted him to make love to Debbie and he also denied wanting Debbie killed because she would not have a lesbian relationship with his girl.

Bardell had then been taken to Salcey Forest with Police Officers in an effort to find the actual scene of the murder but after almost a year was unable to pinpoint where the executions had taken place.

Parkinson, meanwhile, told the investigating detectives that Cox and Fallon had been lured to Salcey Forest and he had stood by as Bardell had killed them. He, Bardell, had stabbed Cox a number of times and had strangled Debbie with a scarf. Both he and Bardell had tried to bury the bodies but the spade they had taken with them had broken.

When the Police asked if Bardell had had sexual intercourse with the dead body of Fallon, Parkinson replied that he had not but had tried to mutilate her body with a knife but it had not been sharp enough so he had ripped off her knickers and kept thém. Parkinson also told the detectives that he had been ordered to murder Ian Turner as he had failed to kill either of the two in Salcey Forest. He had enticed Turner to a field and had stabbed him in the back but had then 'lost his bottle' and could not go through with the killing.

Both men were duly charged and in February 1984 appeared at Northampton Crown Court where they both pleaded not guilty to murdering David Cox and Debbie Fallon and conspiracy to murder Ian Turner.

Mr Desmond Fennel Q.C. led for the Crown and outlined the case to the jury.

One of the first witnesses for the prosecution was Michael Lakin who had lived with Cox and Fallon for a time and he knew Bardell well. He told the Court that Bardell had been keen on the occult and had a ouija board. On occasions, when Bardell had sessions, he had joined in and they had called up the spirit of the ouija and asked it questions. Once Bardell had asked if he and his wife could have another woman come and live with them and the spirit had said it was OK and that if they did not do it then something would happen to their middle child. Lakin added that Bardell was also interested in worshipping the devil and when he had visited Bardell at his home he had seen a number of knives lying on top of a cupboard.

Bardell, Lakin went on, had discussed forming a chapter of the Hell's Angels in Northampton but in his own mind he thought it was nothing more than a childish game and they never did anything more adventurous then go on day trips, although there were plans to take the 'colours' of a chapter in Peterborough. In his opinion, Bardell was 'all mouth' and just wanted people to recognise him as leader.

Sue Turner now went into the witness box. She said that she had come to know Parkinson and Bardell when she became interested in CB radio. She had been rather lonely and had started to talk to the two men over the air quite a lot. Eventually she had met Bardell and by Christmas 1981 had developed a strong feeling for him. He had wanted her to move in with him and although she did not like the idea at first, she had gone to live with him for a trial period. She had also joined the Lucifer's Outlaws and had gone on outings with them to Wickstead Park, Kettering and to Salcey Forest. In May 1982 she decided to go back to her husband and Bardell had been very annoyed and did not understand why she had decided to leave him. She explained that she was still quite fond of him but her children were more important to her. Bardell told her that he loved her and could not understand why she would not live with him. When she persisted, he asked her ominously why he should not kill her and go down for three instead of two.

When she had returned to her husband, they had made plans to go on holiday but on the night before their departure, when they had been putting out posters, Bardell had driven up to them, blocked them in with his car and had emerged in a real temper and armed with a machette. He shouted at her husband, 'Come on Ian, it's you and me!' By standing between them, Sue related, she had managed to calm Bardell down and he drove away after a somewhat tense few minutes.

Whilst on holiday in Skegness she had 'phoned Bardell to tell him that she still loved him. He had replied that he had received a call from the Road Rats telling Bardell that they were not satisfied with the Outlaws and that they wanted three people 'wasting'.

The Turners moved to London and Sue continued to phone Bardell. One day he calmly informed her that he and Parkinson were going to kill Cox and Fallon and that he had to be in London the next day to bring proof to the Road Rats of their murders. He went on that the Rats were angry that Parkinson's girl friend had revealed the whereabouts of an armoury. When Sue had enquired why she was not on the 'hit list', Bardell had explained that he had made a bargain keeping her out of it. He added that if three people were not killed, the Road Rats would come to Northampton and murder all of them.

Next day she had met Bardell at a Greenford public house where he told her that he and Parkinson had met Cox and Fallon at the Weston Favell Centre after telling them that they had found treasure in Salcey Forest. When they had arrived at a secluded spot he had then stabbed Cox to death after Parkinson had failed to kill him. He had then broken Debbie's neck with his bare hands as she pleaded with him not to kill her. Bardell had then shown Sue a photograph that he had taken of the bodies, but it was of such poor quality that in order to prove to the Road Rats that he had carried out two of their demanded executions he had removed Debbie's panties and had brought them. At first, she continued, she could not believe that he had carried out the murders as he seemed so calm and collected but when she had returned to Northampton, she had gone to Bardell's home and expressed some reservations about the murders to Bardell. He had offered to take her to Salcey Forest to show where the bodies were but she had declined the invitation. Bardell had then told her that the third person to be killed on the orders of the Road Rats was her husband Ian! Bardell said that the Turner car would be 'wired up'. A call would be made to Ian asking him to go out and meet Parkinson and when he started up the car it would explode. Needless to say, although the telephone call was made and Ian Turner went off in the car nothing happened and he had returned to the house later that evening somewhat bewildered, as Parkinson had not met him at the designated place. Sue Turner added that after their car had been 'wired', she could not look when her husband drove off to meet Parkinson. When Bardell and Parkinson had examined the car afterwards, neither could understand why the vehicle had failed to explode. When she was cross-examined, she replied that the only relief she felt was when her husband 'phoned her and said that he could not find Steven (Parkinson) and was coming home.

Ian Turner now gave evidence and acknowledged that he knew that his wife had had relationships with other men and he 'encouraged' this. They were both interested in CB radio and it was through this shared interest that they had met Bardell and Parkinson. He became worried about Bardell's friendship towards his wife and when, in 1982, she had gone to live with him he was not speaking to Bardell at all. Later Sue had returned and they had planned a holiday in Skegness but then had come the incident where Bardell had driven up and threatened him with a machette. After they had returned from the holiday Parkinson had phoned him and asked him to meet him again to discuss relations with his wife. (He obviously did not know that the previous meeting had been when his car had been inexpertly 'wired'.) Before he left, Sue had warned him not to turn his back on Parkinson for one second. He had taken his dog and two knives with him. The two men had driven into the country and both had got out of the car and had gone into a field. Despite his wife's warning, when Turner had momentarily turned his back to Parkinson, he had come up and stabbed him. Turner had chased after Parkinson and had demanded to know why had had attacked him. He replied that the Road Rats had ordered his execution. Turner stated that he did not believe this and that he thought Bardell was behind it. Parkinson had come for him again and they had started fighting with knives but Turner had managed to cut his assailant on the chest and back. Parkinson had then got a hammer and a knife but lost them and had returned to the car to fetch a shovel but had fled when Turner had waved his dog lead around. He had called his wife and had gone to Northampton General Hospital for treatment. Sue had visited him with Bardell who told him to keep his mouth shut to which the injured man replied that he would keep the Police out of the matter. He was, he explained, thinking of his wife and children at the time. Bardell later told him that he had been in touch with the Road Rats and they had said that both men should see Mrs Turner two days each week. Bardell also informed Turner that he had murdered Cox and Fallon. As he described the killings to Turner he became very upset and had to leave the room where Turner was recovering, in tears. Turner had stared after him in disbelief.

When he had been discharged from the hospital, Bardell had told him that he and Parkinson had had to pay the Road Rats £500 each because they had not killed Turner.

The next two witnesses added an even more bizarre dimension to the proceedings. John Connelly admitted that he was a member of the Road Rats, a motor-cycle outlaw group and that he went under the alias of Muff. He owned up to having previous convictions for possession of offensive weapons, including an axe and a lemon-squeezer filled with ammonia and to being at a party in Cookham the previous year when a fight had broken out in which two people had died and in connection with which he now faced a charge of criminal affray. He had met Bardell in London but there had never been any conversation between the two men about the deaths in Salcey Forest. He further stated that no group wanting to set up a chapter would need the permission of the Road Rats. Paul Smith, known as Sweet Pea, also admitted knowing Bardell but to his knowledge there had never been any talk of him setting up an Outlaw group.

Detective Constable Roy Neale, of the Thames Valley Police Crime Squad, who had arrested Parkinson, was the next witness. He told the Court that in an interview with his prisoner, Parkinson had mentioned going with Bardell to drugs parties organised by the Hell's Angels. Bardell had discussed setting up a chapter in Northampton with Parkinson playing a leading role but they had to talk the matter over first with the top men of the Road Rats. They wanted to know how often he had been in trouble with the Police and that he should never co-operate with them.

At one stage, in the course of the interview, DC Neale recounted, he had asked Parkinson if he was under any physical threat. Parkinson had put his head in his hands and had started crying. He appeared very distressed. He had told the detective that he was very frightened of the Hells Angels and had added, 'If I tell you why, they will kill me, kill Babs, (the woman Parkinson was living with) and kill the kids.

After Detective Inspector Cusworth had related how he had arrested Bardell and the subsequent interview with him, Superintendent Diccox entered the witness box. The slim, dapper, youthful-looking Police Officer told of the raid at Bardell's home and of the literature the Police had found there. There were books on witchcraft, sadistic sex, pornography and on brutal killings. He had mentioned this to Bardell, 'Do you think that is normal?' he had queried. 'Everything in your lifestyle is connected with violence.' He added that he did not believe that Cox and Fallon had been killed because a London Chapter of the Hell's Angels had demanded the murders because of a mistake by Bardell's own Northampton chapter. 'All the stories were out of your head. The London Road Rats would not be interested in a group of youngsters. You didn't even have motorbikes.' Bardell admitted the murders to the detective, acknowledging that they may have been committed because he was losing face among the others in his chapter.

To a hushed Crown Court, Superintendent Diccox went on to say how Bardell had told him how Parkinson had sat down with him to discuss ways of killing people, and that Parkinson had believed his story about the Hell's Angels demanding the murders. Then, one night in June 1982, Bardell had gone with Parkinson, Cox and Fallon to Salcey Forest. Parkinson had stabbed Cox and had tried to dig a grave for him whilst Debbie Fallon was handcuffed to a tree. Bardell claimed that he had tried to think of a way of saving her but could not, so he had broken her neck with a scarf. This cut no ice with Superintendent Diccox who was satisfied that the stabbing was Bardell's own work. He, however, denied this and continued to blame Parkinson.

Having presented the prosecution's case it now befell the defence to rebut the allegations made against the two men. Accordingly Bardell now exchanged the dock for the witness box. As his counsel led him, Bardell admitted that he derived the greatest enjoyment from boosting his own ego and being the centre of attraction. He had lied to people, he told the court, about being involved in two murders, about being in prison on previous occasions, about being a marksman, an amateur boxer and having a trial with Chelsea Football Club. He had no previous convictions, he was Church of England and he had even played drums for the Salvation Army. Two days before the killings, he related, he had met Parkinson who was, at this time, sharing his home with Cox and Fallon. Parkinson was having an affair with Fallon, but, he informed Bardell, he was fed up with her. He told Bardell that Debbie did not want an affair 'the way he wanted it'. He was going to make sure that Debbie would not mess anyone else around.

On 23rd June 1982, Parkinson had given him a lift to his, Bardell's parents' house, where he had arrived at 7.15pm and he had not left there until 10.15pm. He was able to be so precise because his father was watching the news and he had left when there had been an interval and Parkinson had called back for him. Parkinson, alleged Bardell, had not seemed to be himself. 'Things just didn't seem right.' They had driven to a nearby wood where Parkinson had informed him that he had got rid of Cox and Fallon. 'I've got rid of them permanently,' 'was the way he had actually put it. He said he could prove it by articles he had in his car, one of which was a photograph of Cox's body.

Mr Igor Judge, defending Parkinson, rose and put it to Bardell that he was a proven liar and a good liar. Bardell had to admit that he did not find it difficult to lie if it suited his purpose.

Mr Judge went on, 'You are giving evidence with one aim in mind, to get away with a crime you have committed.'

Bardell responded, 'My purpose is to have the truth come out.'

Earlier, Bardell had alleged that he was dyslexic, having difficulty reading and spelling, but now Mr Judge queried this. 'Who was it who read the books on witchcraft, crime, sadism and Nazism which were found in your house?'

Bardell replied, 'My wife . . . read the witchcraft books. The books on sadism belonged to Ian Turner. I didn't get the chance to read them or to have them read to me.'

'Do you admire Adolf Hitler?' was the next question.

'There are certain aspects that make sense,' was the damning answer from Bardell, who also admitted to being a former member of the November 9th group.

Bardell, under a relentless cross-examination, said that Parkinson had told him that he had taken Cox into Salcey Forest whilst Debbie Fallon had remained in his car. He had, after murdering Cox, fetched her to the spot and had broken her neck. 'I did not know whether to believe Parkinson. I knew he was taking drugs and I thought it was the drugs talking. If I had been a hundred percent certain Parkinson was telling the truth I would have told the Police.'

Not unnaturally, Mr Judge accused Bardell of lying.

'I intended telling the Police when I was arrested but when I was being interviewed my ego built up. I went along with the ego boost.'

When mention was made of Ian Turner, his lover Sue's husband, Bardell told the Crown Court of how he had armed himself up for a duel with him.

'I took two knives and went to see Turner in Earl Street, Northampton, before the Turners set off on holiday in Skegness. I was going to give Ian the opportunity to sort things out with me and not stir trouble behind mine and Sue's backs.'

Bardell was forced to admit that it was possible that someone might have got injured but no duel had taken place because Sue Turner had stepped in to calm things down.

When Mr Fennell Q.C. had asked about claims he had made to the Police that the Road Rats had ordered the killing, Bardell had to agree that these were absolute make believe.

The Court then heard that an attempt had been made by the father of Bardell to persuade a man to give an alibi for his son for the night of the murders. Allan Scarley thought he had seen Bardell on the night of 23rd June 1982 but had to admit that he was not sure of the actual date and Bardell's father had called on him three times and tried to 'put words into his mouth'.

The parents of Bardell had both stated that their son had been with them for the whole of the evening of the fateful day and had carried out a few minor chores.

This concluded the defence case for Bardell and Mr Judge, for Parkinson, decided not to call any evidence.

In his closing speech, Mr Fennell outlined the points that had been raised during the course of the trial adding that Bardell had shown a morbid interest in the murders by collecting all the newspapers with stories about the killings so that he could read what he had done. He described him as a vain little man to whom it was meat and drink to read in the newspapers of his exploits. Mr Fennell added that these murders had been an exercise in power by two aspiring Hell's Angels. Bardell's defence was an alibi which he had produced after the Police had interviewed him and taken statements from him and should be looked at with a good deal of criticism, he advised the jury. Bardell had signed his name sixty-nine times on the pages of the interview notes and had made no fewer than ninety-two corrections but now claimed that his evidence had been taken out of context by the Police. 'Does that,' Mr Fennell enquired, 'sound like somebody who is entitled to say afterwards that it was taken out of context and they got it wrong? Or is it somebody who is having to hedge his bets because he realised the difficulty he was in?' Bardell had given the Police an accurate description of the clothes Cox and Fallon had been wearing when they had died and of how their bodies had been left to lie and Parkinson had played a full and active part in the deaths of Cox and Fallon and also went out to execute a plot to kill Ian Turner. Mr Fennell disputed Parkinson's claim to have acted under duress, adding that there were many occasions that he could have contacted the Police. He had, Mr Fennell went on, played his part in the murders of David Cox and Debbie Fallon in several ways including handcuffing her to a tree. He urged the jury to convict them both.

Mr Judge, in turn, tried to emphasise that Parkinson had been forced to play a part in the killings, whilst Mr Marriage, for Bardell, stressed his client's previous good character and that Parkinson had proved quite capable to stabbing someone.

The trial Judge, Mr Justice Jupp, in addressing the Jury said that both defendants had admitted in Police interviews to planning to kill Ian Turner but Bardell had denied it in Court and they had to be satisfied that the Prosecution had completely negated Bardell's alibi defence.

The Jury were out for seven and a half hours deliberating, before returning with verdicts of guilty against both men on all charges.

Mr Justice Jupp now spoke to the offenders. They were, he said, guilty of quite appalling murders, done entirely in cold blood. They had been planned and carried out with appalling determination. There was absolutely no excuse whatever; jealousy, anger – a motive of this kind seems to be missing in this case and although he was quite satisfied that Parkinson was under the influence of Bardell to a very great extent there was no excuse for joining in murder. Turning to Bardell Mr Jupp said, 'It's perfectly clear you are an evil influence and but for the dreadful influence you spread from your diseased mind, nothing like this would have possibly happened.'

Both men were sentenced to life imprisonment with a recommendation that they should serve no less that twenty years and, for the conspiracy to murder Ian Turner, each was sentenced to ten years imprisonment to run concurrently.

Both men were removed from the Court to begin their sentences for two utterly senseless and motiveless murders.

INDEX

Books Published by
THE BOOK CASTLE

COUNTRYSIDE CYCLING IN BEDFORDSHIRE,
BUCKINGHAMSHIRE AND HERTFORDSHIRE: Mick Payne.
Twenty rides on- and off-road for all the family.   1 871199 92 1

PUB WALKS FROM COUNTRY STATIONS:
Bedfordshire and Hertfordshire: Clive Higgs.Fourteen circular
country rambles, each starting and finishing at a railway station and
incorporating a pub-stop at a mid-way point.   1 871199 53 0

PUB WALKS FROM COUNTRY STATIONS:
Buckinghamshire and Oxfordshire: Clive Higgs.
Circular rambles incorporating pub-stops.   1 871199 73 5

LOCAL WALKS: **North and Mid Bedfordshire:** Vaughan Basham.
Twenty-five thematic circular walks.   1 871199 48 4

FAMILY WALKS: **Chilterns South:** Nick Moon.
Thirty 3 to 5 mile circular walks.   1 871199 38 7

FAMILY WALKS: **Chilterns North:** Nick Moon.
Thirty shorter circular walks.   1 871199 68 9

CHILTERN WALKS: **Hertfordshire, Bedfordshire and**
North Buckinghamshire: Nick Moon.   1 871199 13 1
CHILTERN WALKS: **Buckinghamshire:** Nick Moon.   1 871199 43 3
CHILTERN WALKS: **Oxfordshire and**
West Buckinghamshire: Nick Moon.   1 871199 08 5
A trilogy of circular walks, in association with the Chiltern Society.
Each volume contains 30 circular walks.

OXFORDSHIRE WALKS: **Oxford, the Cotswolds and the**
Cherwell Valley: Nick Moon.   1 871199 78 6
OXFORDSHIRE WALKS: **Oxford, the Downs and**
the Thames Valley: Nick Moon.   1 871199 32 8
Two volumes that complement Chiltern Walks: Oxfordshire and
complete coverage of the county, in association with the Oxford
Fieldpaths Society. Thirty circular walks in each.

JOURNEYS INTO BEDFORDSHIRE: Anthony Mackay.
Foreword by The Marquess of Tavistock, Woburn Abbey. A lavish book
of over 150 evocative ink drawings.   1 871199 17 4

JOURNEYS INTO BUCKINGHAMSHIRE: Anthony Mackay
Superb line drawings plus background text: large format landscape
gift book. 1 871199 14 X

BUCKINGHAMSHIRE MURDERS: Len Woodley
Nearly two centuries of nasty crimes. 1 871199 93 X

**HISTORIC FIGURES IN THE BUCKINGHAMSHIRE
LANDSCAPE:** John Houghton.
Major personalities and events that have shaped the county's past,
including a special section on Bletchley Park. 1 871199 63 8

TWICE UPON A TIME: John Houghton. 1 871199 09 3
Short stories loosely based on fact, set in the North Bucks area.

**MANORS and MAYHEM, PAUPERS and PARSONS: Tales from
Four Shires: Beds., Bucks., Herts., and Northants.:** John Houghton
Little-known historical snippets and stories. 1 871199 18 2

**MYTHS and WITCHES, PEOPLE and POLITICS: Tales from Four
Shires: Bucks., Beds., Herts., and Northants.:** John Houghton.
Anthology of strange, but true historical events. 1 871199 82 4

**FOLK: Characters and Events in the History of Bedfordshire and
Northamptonshire:** Vivienne Evans.
Anthology about people of yesteryear – arranged alphabetically by
village or town. 1 871199 25 5

JOHN BUNYAN: His Life and Times: Vivienne Evans.
Highly-praised and readable account. 1 871199 87 5

THE RAILWAY AGE IN BEDFORDSHIRE: Fred Cockman.
Classic, illustrated account of early railway history. 1 871199 22 0

**GLEANINGS REVISITED: Nostalgic Thoughts of a Bedfordshire
Farmer's Boy:** E W O'Dell. 1 871199 77 8
His own sketches and early photographs adorn this lively account of
rural Bedfordshire in days gone by.

FARM OF MY CHILDHOOD, 1925–1947: Mary Roberts.
An almost vanished lifestyle on a remote farm near Flitwick. 1 871199 50 6

BEDFORDSHIRE'S YESTERYEARS Vol 2: The Rural Scene:
Brenda Fraser-Newstead. 1 871199 47 6
Vivid first-hand accounts of country life two or three generations ago.

**BEDFORDSHIRE'S YESTERYEARS Vol 3: Craftsmen and
Tradespeople:** Brenda Fraser-Newstead.
Fascinating recollections over several generations practising many
vanishing crafts and trades. 1 871199 03 4

BEDFORDSHIRE'S YESTERYEARS Vol 4:
War Times and Civil Matters: Brenda Fraser-Newstead.
Two World Wars, plus transport, law and order, etc.   1 871199 23 9

DUNSTABLE IN TRANSITION: 1550-1700:
Vivienne Evans.   1 871199 98 0
Wealth of original material as the town evolves without the Priory.

DUNSTABLE WITH THE PRIORY: 1100-1550: Vivienne Evans.
Dramatic growth of Henry I's important new town around a major
crossroads.   1 871199 56 5

DUNSTABLE DECADE: THE EIGHTIES:
A Collection of Photographs: Pat Lovering.
A souvenir book of nearly 300 pictures of people and events in the
1980s.   1 871199 35 2

DUNSTABLE IN DETAIL: Nigel Benson.   09509773 2 2
A hundred of the town's buildings and features, plus town trail map.

OLD DUNSTABLE: Bill Twaddle.
A new edition of this collection of early photographs.   1 871199 05 0

BOURNE and BRED:
A Dunstable Boyhood Between the Wars:
Colin Bourne.
An elegantly written, well-illustrated book capturing the spirit of the
town over fifty years ago.   1 871199 40 9

ROYAL HOUGHTON: Pat Lovering:
Illustrated history of Houghton Regis from the earliest times to the
present.   0 9509773 1 4

THE STOPSLEY BOOK: James Dyer.
Definitive, detailed account of this historic area of Luton. 150 rare
photographs.   h/b – 1 871199 24 7; p/b – 1 871199 04 2

THE CHANGING FACE OF LUTON: An Illustrated History:
Stephen Bunker, Robin Holgate and Marian Nichols.
Luton's development from earliest times to the present busy
industrial town. Illustrated in colour and mono.
     h/b – 1 871199 66 2; p/b – 1 871199 71 9

THE MEN WHO WORE STRAW HELMETS:
Policing Luton, 1840-1974: Tom Madigan..
Meticulously chronicled history; dozens of rare photographs; author
served in Luton Police for fifty years.
     h/b – 1 871199 81 6; p/b – 1 871199 11 5
                                                                    •

BETWEEN THE HILLS:
The Story of Lilley, a Chiltern Village:
Roy Pinnock.   1 871199 02 6
A priceless piece of our heritage – the rural beauty remains but the
customs and way of life described here have largely disappeared.

KENILWORTH SUNSET:
A Luton Town Supporter's Journal:
Tim Kingston.
Frank and funny account of football's ups and downs.   1 871199 83 2

A HATTER GOES MAD!:
Kristina Howells.   1 871199 58 1
Luton Town footballers, officials and supporters talk to a female fan.

LEGACIES: Tales and Legends of Luton and the North Chilterns:
Vic Lea.
Twenty-five mysteries and stories based on fact, including Luton
Town Football Club. Many photographs.   1 8711199 91 3

LEAFING THROUGH LITERATURE:
Writers' Lives in Hertfordshire and Bedfordshire: David Carroll.
Illustrated short biographies of many famous authors and their
connections with these counties.   .   1 871199 01 8

A PILGRIMAGE IN HERTFORDSHIRE: H M Alderman.
Classic, between-the-wars tour round the county, embellished with
line drawings.   1 871199 33 6

SUGAR MICE AND STICKLEBACKS:
Childhood Memories of a Hertfordshire Lad: Harry Edwards
Vivid evocation of those gentler pre-war days in an archetypal
village, Hertingfordbury.   1 871199 88 3

SWANS IN MY KITCHEN: Lis Dorer.
Story of a Swan Sanctuary near Hemel Hempstead.   1 871199 62 X

THE HILL OF THE MARTYR:
An Architectural History of St. Albans Abbey: Eileen Roberts.
Scholarly and readable chronological narrative history of
Hertfordshire and Bedfordshire's famous cathedral. Fully illustrated
with photographs and plans. h/b – 1 871199 21 2; p/b – 1 871199 26 3

CHILTERN ARCHAEOLOGY: RECENT WORK:
A Handbook for the Next Decade:
edited by Robin Holgate.
The latest views, results and excavations by twenty-three leading
archaeologists throughout the Chilterns.   1 871199 52 2

THE TALL HITCHIN SERGEANT:
A Victorian Crime Novel Based on Fact: Edgar Newman.
Mixes real police officers and authentic background with an exciting
storyline.   1 871199 07 7

THE TALL HITCHIN INSPECTOR'S CASEBOOK:
A Victorian Crime Novel Based on Fact: Edgar Newman.
Worthies of the time encounter more archetypal villains. 1 871199 67 0

SPECIALLY FOR CHILDREN

VILLA BELOW THE KNOLLS: A Story of Roman Britain:
Michael Dundrow.
An exciting adventure for young John in Totternhoe and Dunstable
two thousand years ago.   1 871199 42 5

THE RAVENS: One Boy Against the Might of Rome:
James Dyer.   1 871199 60 3
On the Barton Hills and in the south-east of England as the men of
the great fort of Ravensburgh (near Hexton) confront the invaders.

Books Distributed by THE BOOK CASTLE

Pictorial Guide to
   Bedfordshire .... Meadows / Larkman 0900804 10 6
Old Bedfordshire .... Houfe 0900804 15 7
The Story of Bedford .... Godber 0900804 24 6
Pictorial Guide to Hertfordshire .... Meadows .... 0900804 22 x
The Story of St. Albans .... Toms 0900804 28 9
History of Milton Keynes, vol 1 .... Markham 0900804 29 7
History of Milton Keynes, vol 2 .... Markham 0900804 30 0
Old Aylesbury .... Viney / Nightingale 0900804 21 1
Village Schooldays and Beyond,
   1906–23 .... Chapman 0951821717
Claydon .... Chapman 0951821709

Further titles are in preparation.
All the above are available via any bookshop, or from the publisher and bookseller,
THE BOOK CASTLE
12 Church Street, Dunstable, Bedfordshire, LU5 4RU
Tel: (01582) 605670